Stupid Cupid!

A Survivor's Guide to Online Dating

By Alison O'Donnell

SR
Stillwater
River

First Stillwater River Publications Edition

Library of Congress Control Number: 2017951316

ISBN-10: 1-946-30025-X
ISBN-13: 978-1-946-30025-6

1 2 3 4 5 6 7 8 9 10
Written by Alison O'Donnell
Cover art by Jamie Forgetta
Cover design by Dawn M. Porter
Published by Stillwater River Publications, Glocester, RI, USA.

Dedication

This book is dedicated to… Me!

That's right, I'm dedicating this book to myself,

because I've paid my dues and deserve the kudos!

I also dedicate this book to all who have painstakingly

sought out a partner in this twisted world

who won't drive them insane. Admit it — it's all so CRAZY!

I would be remiss if I didn't also include my late dad,

a Marine, who taught me nearly everything

I know about men.

Semper Fi, Daddy! ♥

Love looks not with the eyes, but with the mind;
and therefore is winged Cupid painted blind.

~ William Shakespeare

Table of Contents

Prologue

You know that scene in *Silence of the Lambs* when the creepy guy, Buffalo Bill, says, "It places the lotion in the basket"? I'm not easily creeped out, but that guy sure got to me. There have been lots of 'creepers', as my teen daughter would call them, in the dating arena. After meeting more than my fair share of them via online ad dates (I've been on at least a hundred over the years, and consider myself somewhat of an authority on the subject at this point), I decided it was high time I wrote a book about it. This book *needed* to come out, and it's been a long time in the making! While it took me two years to put it all together, the dates themselves span over 30 years. In all that time, not much has changed.

As they say in the world of comedy, "This stuff writes itself!" The stories are all true—I could never, in a bahzillion years, make this stuff up if I tried!! Of course, the commentary that follows each story was written off the top of my head, and you get the benefit of gleaning what I learned from each date. I can laugh about them now, but at the time there was a painful lesson to be learned from each. Today, I am grateful for that.

The first time someone asked me what my book is about, without thinking I blurted, "It's a self-help comedy of horrors!" I actually toyed with putting that in the title, but nobody would use search words like those to find a book on dating advice! (I also wanted to misspell Stoopid in the title, but my publisher talked me out of it for the same reason.) It's a touchy subject for many,

1

including me, and so I'd been very private about it all. I also didn't want the idea stolen. Been there… (More on that later).

I'm sure there are lots of other women out there (and men!) who've had similar dating experiences and thought to write about it. In fact, whenever I told people I was writing a book about the horrors of online dating, they'd almost always light up and say, "Oh, I've been thinking about doing that too! I have SO many stories!" I happen to be an English teacher, editor and stand-up comedian, so it seemed only fitting that I should actually *get 'er done*. Here it is; I hope you like it. You'll see yourself in some of these pages, or maybe just laugh along as you go. It's prolly more of a chick book, but I think guys will learn a lot by reading it too. Think of it as a handy guide. I might be able to help get you to a second date, but the rest is on you!

Oh yeah — every guy who found out I was a comedian then said, "Wow, are you gonna talk about our date in your act? Haha!" (*Guffaw!*) Ah, no. However, I must change some names here to protect the (not-so) innocent. You understand. They never thought they'd end up lampooned in a book, did they? I've given them creative names instead, which helped me to catalogue them as I went along. I think you'll enjoy the foreshadowing this offers.

All misspellings are intentional. Call it me being a rebellious English teacher/editor/comedian. I grew up in a very tough neighborhood, but I attended a parochial school so I got the best of both worlds — an excellent education in and outside of school. You may also notice an intentional flop in writing style, sometimes sounding educated, sometimes sounding "ghetto". This is who I am at the core. You can take the girl out of the ghetto, but you can't take the ghetto out of the girl. There you have it — streetwise author!

One more disclaimer: I'm not perfect. While it may seem I'm picking on some (OK, most) of these people, it's true (at least from my perspective) that they had issues which prevented them from having successful relationships. It's easy to hide behind a computer screen if you're painfully shy, not good with dating or with women in general, or are lacking in the social graces. I'm calling them out here. No doubt if you talked to these men, you'd get an earful about *me*. To this, all I can do is remind you, gentle reader, that there are two sides to every story. If they want to tell theirs, they'll just have to write their own @#$!% book! It's time consuming, but I enjoyed every minute of this project, and mebbe even found it to be cathartic. I've made it my mission, in my (sometimes very) candid purging, to help you daters everywhere to prepare for the inevitable crappy experiences you will encounter. It's that whole "Gotta kiss a bunch of toads before you find your prince" and finding the proverbial needle in a haystack thing. Learn from my mistakes. Or, if you're just reading this for the entertainment value, welcome to my nightmare! Live vicariously through my comedy of horrors and errors! Mebbe you'll read something that resonates with you. If you've been at this a while, as I have, you will likely find yourself nodding furiously!

My tales end with a moral — a lesson to be learned that I pre-learned for you and freely share here in the hopes that you may one day find happiness in love. You don't have to agree with everything I say here. It's my name on the book, my (sarcastic) humble opinion you're getting. It's OK to disagree, especially when your experiences have been different. Remember, I'm coming into this with a biased slant. I hope that I'm helping you to weed out the riff raff, the psychos, the cellar dwellers... *I am a comedian, and never apologize for finding the humor in all things!* If we can't laugh at ourselves... There's value in my pessimistic view because of (its comedic gold) my bad experiences, but I fully admit that it *can* happen — you just might find love online! Serendipity is a thing! Go forth and date-apply. Good luck!

Types of Men

I 'm sure I've forgotten far more crazy dates than I've listed here, and the book would be much fatter if only my brain were more cooperative, but this is what I was able to come up with — the ones that *really* stuck with me. After all, gotta strike while the iron's hot! Dating ads have advanced from newspapers and booklets found in laundromats, to the online digital format of today. Online dating is the single most popular way for singles to meet other singles today! Who knows what's next? Can't keep this book in my computer forever; it needs to be let out before teleporting becomes real!

The memories came to me in no particular order, but I did put the non-digital ones upfront, in chronological order. It just makes sense that you see how patient, learned and perseverant I got as I matured over the years (ahem).

Before I introduce you to them individually, there are some 'types' you should know about. I've managed to categorize them once I recognized patterns. It's like the Whack a Mole game at a carnival. Walk tall, and carry a big hammer! Here they are...

Houdini

This is what I call the men who seemed SO interested, and then, without warning, *POOF!* They simply *disappeared!* (Women do this too!) This is so common, in fact, that it's been given the official term of *ghosting*. My theory is that most people online are talking to about five other people while they're pretending to be so interested in you. It's only fair that you do the same. I don't mean disappear — that's rude! — but keep your options open while learning more about each person. You don't have to be a serial dater, but you're not committed to anyone at the moment and are free to date as many people as you'd like. You *should* keep your options open until you find some*one* you want to spend your time with. Just don't string someone else along who's really interested in you. Let him/her know you two are *just talking* (and dating others!). They may choose not to continue with you, since clearly you are not totally into them when they are looking to be monogamous, but it's the right thing to do.

That's a sign of a healthy person — someone who will not let himself/herself be used, or be back-burner material. They are looking for a commitment, and won't settle for less. Good for them! Nobody's settling! You know what you want, so go for it. Do not allow yourself to be placed on the back burner by someone who isn't really interested! Sometimes it's hard to know for sure. Games are played, lies are told. It happens. Stay vigilant. If s/he is truly interested, s/he isn't going anywhere.

I think what happens is that we tend to lean toward one person in particular, and don't want to confuse things by dating more than one person, so we let the others go. You disappear on their end, forgetting to contact them (or think you don't need to). And when things don't go so well with the one you thought you'd click with, you feel like you can't go back (three months later) and contact those others. Like you, they've moved on.

Be assured — Houdinis have others in the wings — people they think are "a sure thing". Or, they know they can't measure up. Mebbe they look nothing like their 10-year-old pic. Mebbe they're married and can't go beyond the texting phase. There are a host of reasons why a person might disappear. It's not you! An honorable person would follow through. Once they've ghosted, show's over folks! Move along, nothing to see here!!

Reappearing Houdinis

Oh sure, some men did try that on me. I actually might've been receptive to talking again if only they hadn't used bogus lines like, "I lost your number but just found it!" Helloooo, you could've contacted me via the online dating site where you originally found me. Our ads are both still active, duh! Do you really think I'm *that* stoopid?!

You may never know why the person went *POOF!* but you don't have to take it personally. The Houdinis of the dating world don't deserve your time. Their loss, move on, *it's not you!*

All you really have to do is be honest. Is that so hard? OK, for some people it really is hard to be honest. It doesn't have to be. If your goal is not to hurt the other person, you just have to know what to say in advance that won't be hurtful. Say something like, "I started dating someone else (Beware — that's a classic blow-off line for cowards who aren't interested in you!), so I'm just going to wish you well and say goodbye." But no, they prefer the *POOF!* approach. It's inconsiderate, and if you do this you can forget about ever contacting that person again! While it's wrong to ask someone to wait for you on the back burner while you feel out this other relationship, there's nothing wrong with popping in three months down the road IF you ended things diplomatically. "Hi, I find myself free again, and see that your ad is still active, so I'm wondering if you'd still be interested in that cup of coffee." Not so hard, really! The worst that can happen is s/he says no. Nothing lost, and now you know.

There are lots of jaded people out there, tired of the dating games after taking a few whacks to the head and heart. You can't blame them, really. If more people were just upfront about what they're thinking and feeling, we could avoid all that. People appreciate honesty after being lied to so often! I've actually had men *thank* me for telling them I wasn't feeling it between us! But since we can't change people, all we can do is protect ourselves. We keep our guard high, waiting for the other foot to fall each time we get our hopes up with someone new. The choice is yours. If you're in a position where there's nothing else happening and you want to give Reappearing Houdini a second chance, go ahead and do it — If the person didn't string you along! Otherwise, you can bet s/he will only do it again. That's a character flaw you don't want to reintroduce into your life.

The Psychotic

Some of these people are just plain nutz. More than once I've lost interest in a man and politely moved on, but in their rejected state they felt the need to send me texts telling me how 'rotten' I am, etc. I won't use the choice words here, but I'm sure you can guess. It took all my strength not to text back, "NO WONDER you're alone! Sheesh!!"

I always hated that feeling of leaving a coffee date knowing I'm right back to the drawing board. One more time waster. Try not to look at it that way though. Before each date, I'd have a little conversation with myself. "This is *just a date*. You are just meeting a potential new friend and seeing where, if anywhere, it goes. It could be a nice person who simply teaches you a lesson you need right now, a new activity pal, or it could be something *really* special! Embrace it all with an open heart and mind, and be grateful for the lesson." Every date is an unknown. It could be a total flop, it could be a one-sided flop, or it could be one more person you'll never see again who got your life story. And then it's *Poof!* all over again, but at least it was done tactfully. With all the single people out there, the chances of you meeting "The One" right off the bat are slim to nil. Be gracious until you find your One (If there is such a thing. My friend Todd says, "With seven billion people on the planet, there's prolly more than one person you can get along with!").

I've no doubt some of the Houdinis are married and just want to have that someone fun to text with during lonely and/or horny moments. Some may even snag you in and *then* admit they're married, hoping you'll take that bait into an affair now that you're hooked. (Nothing surprises me anymore!) To those sexting user losers, I say, "That will be $3.99 per minute. The charges begin now!"

The Lurkers

These folks run their ads (usually on more than one site) for well over a year. When they see that you are currently looking, after having snubbed them last year and taken a break, they will write again in hopes that you (are now willing to settle) will think they're a new member (despite the fact they're using the same old photos), or will now give them a chance since you are still out there looking too.

If you don't find that oddly scary, you should! It reeks of desperation.

The Stuck

People get stuck in life. Stuck on their ex's, stuck in their ruts, immobile in an otherwise changing world. It's OK to feel sorry for these types, but it is not your job to fix them! It rarely works anyway. If you are truly ready for a relationship, you will *be physically and emotionally available to give yourself to a partner in all ways.* Don't you deserve the same? If it's a healthy relationship you seek — one that is mutually rewarding — then the answer is a resounding YES! This is why I won't even entertain the idea of dating someone whose marital status is listed as separated — You're still married!! Go settle your unfinished business, then we can talk!

If you are feeling the urge to 'fix' the person, if you are making his/her drama *your* problem, go buy a self-help book on codependency. Read it twice. (Seriously!! I highly recommend *Codependent No More* by Melody Beattie) Men tend to be fixers, want to play the hero/savior role. And women are innately compassionate, playing mommy to old boys who will never grow up. Turn away from other people's drama and satisfy *your* needs. Take care of self. I'm not saying run when things get tough in your partner's life, but if you're walking into a hornet's nest at the get-go, it ain't gonna work in the long run (keyword: RUN!).

Picture Senders

Guys — FYI, most women do NOT want a photo of your junk! Sure, there are plenty out there who would be receptive, and even send you a nudie of themselves first, but if you think she's a keeper, be a decent guy about it. IF things are progressing in that direction, ASK first. IF the lady says no, DON'T SEND IT! At least be smart enough to send one with no face showing, so that when it goes viral, your life is still relatively intact. Personally, I find those photos offensive. We are not yet intimate — that's a slow-building thing — so when you send me a pic of your anatomy that I did not pre-approve or request, it's very clear to me you're only looking for one thing (and have no class, or Asperger's). How about instead of sending me nudies, send a pic of the inside of your medicine cabinet. At least then I know what else I'm dealing with here! Otherwise, NEXT!!

I'm AMAZED at how many men have sent me unsolicited shots of their erect penis (assuming it actually was theirs in the pic. They were smart enough to chop their head off; no pun intended). I tell my friends that, if it continues, I'll have enough pics of men's junk to create a coffee table book! C'mon guys, SERIOUSLY?! If you can't find something better to do on a Friday night, you will prolly always be alone! Just sayin'. Although, I'm told women can be just as bad, sending nude selfies of their chests, etc. Hey, if that's your thing, go for it, but it's not going to attract a classy mate.

Always put your best foot forward! YOU be the one with your head held high when you part company. No need to air your dirty laundry, or pics, before or at a first meeting!!

While on the subject of sending pictures, beware of those who ask you to send! This is an automatic turn-off to me. You've already seen at least three good shots of me, and you're dating me, not my pic! Have enough class to agree to meet the person based upon the pics you've seen, hoping for the best. If the posted pics are old and PhotoShopped, why would you think this person just snapped a picture now for your sake?!

Young Men

"Not sure why they want to see my vagina at this age considering they could've seen it from the inside coming out!" says my comedian bud, Liani. But I get it... Young men want to try the cougar thing. Free sex with a horny older oh-so-appreciative woman who knows more tricks and has less inhibitions than the younger ladies. I'm sure there are women out there who would jump at the chance to (teach) hook up with virile young men, but that's not even necessarily a guarantee of quality sex, never mind finding love there. Actually, because women statistically live longer — about eight years longer than men — it makes sense for a woman to seek out a man a bit her junior. However, if you are old enough to have diapered him yourself, it's prolly best to thank him for the compliment, then tell him sorry but, "I have refrigerated leftovers older than you! Run along now — your mommy's calling!"

Of course there are men looking for much younger women for the same reason, and there are young women who would accept them or seek them out. I have two theories on this one. Either the young woman has daddy issues, in which case she needs someone to coddle her because Daddy didn't. She wants someone to take care of her. Or, she is looking for someone to take care of her *financially*. It's OK to be a sugar daddy if you are so willing. Nobody can take advantage of you without your permission. If this works for you, it's a win/win! It doesn't seem like a healthy relationship to me, but who am I to judge? People partner up for different reasons, and if both people are getting what they want out of the arrangement, it works! <Shrug>

Name-44-Town
Plenty of Toads

My cell phone is loaded with contacts that look like this. You never know if a Houdini will reappear, be a loser who doesn't realize he'd already contacted you six months earlier, or turn out to be your doctor… Arranging my potential suitors in this way (his name, age, location, dating site) allows me to manage them all, so when they call I have a good idea of whom I'm talking to! Keeping track of who's who can get overwhelming after you've talked with many people, especially when your ad is new, and especially if you're utilizing more than one site. Everyone loves fresh meat, and you will get bombarded with responses in the beginning. Having a system is paramount, lest you feel like an idiot when you answer the call, "Hello, who's this?" Needless to say, it's a turnoff to your potential suitor as it screams "I've got a few of you going right now and can't keep 'em all straight!" Try to keep 'em all straight. Nobody wants to be called by the wrong name, and you appear much sharper and worthy if you show interest. In the early days, I kept a diary of notes on each person. This allowed me to remember specifics on the men so I didn't have to ask them their life story all over again. It just makes sense! It is a lot of work though. At this point, I don't remember who half of them are. But I'll have a pretty good idea if they drunk call me at 2am!

Additionally, this system comes in really handy if you have a friend who is also playing with the ads. Sometimes your friend will come across someone you've already spoken to and you can refer back to your diary to share notes. "Oh yeah, Fisherman69?* Named Paul? He was a loser, talked about himself for 10 minutes before I bailed. Plus he has six young kids with five different women... Run!"

*Their chosen screen name is often very telltale of who they (think they) are!

The Braggarts

Beware those who brag. It's a confidence thing, or lack thereof. They're never as good as they claim to be — they're just convincing themselves they are! In need of ego stroking, they do it for themselves.

If he's already bragging about how good he is in the sack, that's a red flag waving! People who *know* they're good don't need to brag. Hopefully, you like them enough to wait it out and find out because you're worth it, not because they said they are. Kind of like a soldier who doesn't talk about what he's seen in combat; he knows he was a good soldier but he wouldn't dream of talking about it (except mebbe with other soldiers). Being willing to please is not the same thing as being able.

Must be nice being you, Mr. Perfect!

The Men

llow me to introduce you to the men who've shaped my thinking. As you know, I've given them all pet names, partly for their protection, partly to help me remember who's who, and also because, well, if the shoe fits…

There is a flow to all this. Going out of order can mess you up. It's like wearing your Monday panties on Saturday.

Dad

No, of course I didn't date my dad. A woman's father is technically the first man in her life though. This is what my dad told me when I graduated high school, "So I wanted to be the first to give you a diamond. I'm so proud of you for finishing school." Not that I wouldn't have finished, I was as nerdy as I was cool in school, but I was touched by the sentiment and diamond initial ring nonetheless. He himself was a high school dropout, not scholastically bright but well-schooled in the ways of the world and how people operate. I learned a lot about men from my very blunt father. He'd share tips with me, never holding back for the sake of decorum. He even encouraged free love, so long as I was safe about it ("If a guy wants to have sex with you, it's up to him to provide the place. Never bring him to your place! You may not want him to find you later!"). Despite him being Protestant, I was raised a good Catholic girl — complete with the obligatory guilt — and would've felt too whorish having commitment-less sex. Still, I hung on Dad's every word, learning how men think, and it has saved me a lot of guesswork over the years!

I was a young bride and recognized early on that I'd made a big mistake. The first year of marriage was great, kids playing house. But the second... Let's just say he'd fallen seriously short on the partner scale once $h!t got real. One day I went to Dad and asked, "I said forever. He's a nice guy, how can I leave him?" My dad, who did not believe in divorce as a rule, casually said to me, "There are a lot of nice men in the world. You don't have to marry

26

them all!" Those words, initially comical, hit me like a ton of bricks — so much so that today I constantly hear them as a sort of mantra for not settling.

More than once I've heard men say, "What's wrong with Average Joe? Why won't women give us nice guys a chance?" There's nothing wrong with Average Joe, he's just better suited to Plain Jane — and needs to give *her* a chance! That ain't me, babe!

Perhaps the most helpful thing Dad taught me was simply put. "Alison, all men are pigs! But you can't fault them for it. This is nature, how God intended it. Otherwise, the species would die out. You don't have to like it but you do have to accept it. *You can't blame a guy for trying!*"

Pennywise

My first ad date ever was when I was 19. Back then, since computers were not yet a household item and photos were expensive to print, ads did not always include pictures. Only those confident in their appearance and finances took on that extra expense. We were willing to risk it though, since our own ad likely didn't include a pic (and women typically aren't as shallow as men. There, I said it).

I was hot, but for whatever reason, men weren't approaching me, and in my loneliness I turned to the dating page of a local newspaper to meet my first in a long line of potential suitors. I'll call him Pennywise, for reasons you'll understand in just a bit.

His ad didn't include a photo. As mentioned, this was the norm back then, lucky for him as he looked like he'd been caught in an elevator that crushed his caveman face around his small mouth. It was so tiny, his teeth were all overlapped on this tiny gum line in an even tinier orifice.

He said he was a lawyer. Score, right? Wrong! He'd just passed the Bar—after three attempts — and hadn't actually had a case yet. That's why he was still living with his mom... He was 28, or so he said (people lie about their age — and height — all the time on these things! What a bad idea, starting out with a lie, especially since the person is going to figure it out fast when you meet and change in height! I've actually had people argue their height with me! How can you claim to be taller when I'm looking down at you?! Your height wasn't a big issue until you lied about it!!).

We'd met for coffee at lunchtime and, when the bill came, it was clear he was only paying for *his* half. That's fine, I never expect anything going into these meetings*, which technically aren't dates at all. (The cheap men will remind me, "This is just a meeting! IF we hit it off, THEN we will have a date!") I was, however, taken back a bit by the large plastic baggie of coins he produced. OK, they were pennies — all pennies! I placed my cash on the table and couldn't get out of there fast enough. However, when he tried to open his baggie to count his change, it burst and pennies poured all over the place! The noise caught the attention of everyone in the joint, and all eyes were on me like the babysitter taking her charge home before the circus ended. A different person might've run, but I felt obligated to get on the floor to help him pick up his change. He said not one word. I prolly should have sprinted, but since I didn't, he asked if he could call me again <sigh>. I was too (stoopid) kind to say I really wasn't interested.

Later that afternoon, Pennywise called from court, all excited. His first case!! Then he called again, five minutes later. "Yeah, we're almost in court, haven't been called in yet." And then he called five minutes later and said, "Still waiting…" Then he called ten minutes after that to tell me how proud of him his mom was! "Yeah, still waiting. Going to be called in any minute now!!" I took that opportunity to let him know I didn't think this was going to work out (which was HUGE for me because I was so non-confrontational back then, always staying quiet so as not to inadvertently hurt anyone's feelings. If this sounds like you, get that codependency self-help book!). His immediate response was, "Yeah, I don't like you either. But, tell me, what is it about me you don't like?" Ugh! Awkward!! I can't…

My, how I've grown since then! No shame in being upfront at the end of the meeting. Why waste your time and theirs? We're all adults here (even those who live with their mommy.

And guys who love their moms are not typically misogynistic, which is a good thing). Repeat after me: There's absotively nothing wrong with politely saying, "It was nice meeting you! Take care!" IF they should persist, very calmly smile and say something like, "Sorry, I'm just not feeling the chemistry here. Good luck in your search." Don't leave even a hint that you'd be open to another phone call — not unless you wouldn't mind keeping him/her around in the friend zone. Nothing wrong with that either. Sometimes we click in personality, it's just not a romantic connection. IF they are interested in being more than friends and you're not, you've gotta spell that out for them in no uncertain terms, since there are none so deaf as those who don't want to hear!

* While I don't mind paying for my coffee or even my half of the dinner tab, I think it's admirable to let the man pay if that's how he was raised. Let him be the chivalrous gentleman if he offers! They want to feel manly, show you they can be the provider, and treat you with the respect you deserve. It can be confusing these days, with some women asserting their independence and insisting on paying for themselves. In that case, what man is going to argue with her?

Regarding ladies paying for anything, my friends say absolutely not! They tell me that "You must treat yourself as the queen the men need to treat you as! Always expect the gentleman to pay. If he just wants to buy you coffee — or worse, makes you pay for your coffee — it's a red flag that he will never treat you right." Men, I know this can get expensive for you, especially if you are a serial dater. Food for thought in choosing your dates wisely, after spending enough time on the phone (You can learn a lot by speaking first! Save yourself the drive if you're not feeling the chemistry over the phone!) before agreeing to meet (just don't let the timeframe drag on past two weeks). Don't worry — once things heat up, your woman will gladly share the tab and occasionally treat!

Nice thing about a cup of coffee, you don't waste an hour on someone who doesn't deserve your time. Unless you're into spending time getting to know folks who could become a new friend, don't feel bad excusing yourself after only ten minutes. You've committed to that much. Beyond that, it's 11+ minutes of your life you can't get back. You don't even have to make excuses why you have to leave! No need to be rude, no need to lie, but don't hesitate to stand and say your polite but firm goodbye, be glad you dodged a bullet, and be on your merry way. If you leave any room for doubt about your disinterest, you could be getting a phone call later.

You can see why I named this clown Pennywise. If I were smart, the lesson here would have been to give up ad dating right there and then, but I figured it could only get better from here. Yeah…

Yugo, I Go!

I should have predicted it would be a nightmare, the date from Hell. I was still so new to ad dating, and didn't quite trust my instincts yet. The only reason I even accepted the date was because I feared the one time I didn't accept, that's when Prince Charming would have gotten away!

Everything was fine over the phone. I really thought there was a chance here. For two weeks we conversed regularly, getting to know what the other person was all about. We just couldn't seem to get our schedules together, so I eagerly awaited our first meeting. He described himself as intelligent, very handsome, tall, blonde and muscular. RI being a very small state where everyone knows everyone else, my cousin was acquainted with him and vouched for him, so I gave him directions to my house (Mistake #1!) and waited. And waited…

Something must have happened, I thought, because the directions were simple enough: After exiting the freeway, count six lights and make a right. When the phone rang, I knew he'd gotten lost, and entertained the thought that mebbe my self-described intelligent friend had no common sense.

He was calling from the next city over. No problem, I tried telling myself, he's nervous and just lost count of the lights. I waited patiently, fantasizing of an air-conditioned restaurant while I boiled inside my house on the hottest day that summer.

Half an hour later, he pulled up in a Yugo. I mention the Yugo because this man was very tall. Imagine my first impression when he rolled up all huddled in this little car. All 6'4" of him was stuffed into this tiny babe magnet — yet he refused to get out of the car because my dog was loose outside. Gizmo was an 11-lb. loveable lickster, complete with a happy tail, so all I could say was, "Are you serious?!"

He was serious. I held onto Giz as the gray-haired blimp ran into my house (Broken rule #2, you don't meet a stranger at your house, and certainly shouldn't let the stranger in!). I followed him inside, where he presented me with a bottle of wine and sat right down. I was dumbfounded. After a minute he said, "Well aren't you going to get me a glass a wine?" I'm usually a fine hostess, but I was starving, my makeup was melting and I was still dreaming of a little AC. I thought I'd die. I fetched the wine just the same.

When I handed the glass of wine to him, he put his feet up on the coffee table and said, "Nice place you've got here," sloshing the wine all over my couch as he motioned the words. I thought, alcoholic, grimacing to myself as I politely thanked him for the compliment.

After an hour of watching Yugo play with the television remote, I suggested we go to the restaurant. He insisted I drive. Thinking it couldn't get any more bizarre than this, I agreed (Broken rule #3, ALWAYS take your own car! You never know when you're going to be stuck at their mercy. Don't do it! Allow for the quick get-away!). To my utter amazement, he took the glass of wine with him, sloshing it all over my car as I drove on abashed.

Once we were in the restaurant, he ordered a drink — at the bar. I gazed in awe as he pulled a crumpled wad of bills out of his pocket. He spread them out across the little high-top bar table and semi-unfolded each one to see what denomination it was. After taking a tally he announced, "Well, I don't have enough for dinner, but we could get a few drinks!" Yup, alcoholic. If there was any doubt, I was now certain.

He held an impressive conversation with the bartender, so I could see he actually was intelligent. After we drank all he could, I drove us back to my house. I was very uncomfortable with the idea of letting him back in my home, and he wasn't ready to leave, so I suggested we go for a walk. It started to sprinkle, and I was thanking baby Jesus for the cool mist when I heard little whimpers coming from my date. "We have to go back. I'm getting wet," he whined. Funny, I was so hot the droplets were just sizzling off of me! We had gone a whopping five houses down the street and he was already wimping out. I wasn't surprised.

Back at my house, he said he didn't like to drive in the rain, and I didn't want him driving under the influence, so I felt obligated to let him in. Very bad idea, but I made sure to sit in the recliner so he couldn't get next to me. Gizmo lovingly lay near his feet. To this he said, "Could you lock your dog up? He's annoying me." I wasn't about to banish my beloved pet from his favorite spot and confine him for this guy's sake, so I called Giz over to lay near me. I then observed my smirking date pat the seat next to him, inviting me over. Ugh.

"It's a little hot to cuddle," said I in my infinite wisdom, "Don't you think?" To this, he rose — and wordlessly walked out the door (Praise Allah)!

"Leaving so soon?" I asked.

Clearly, this was not a love match. No words needed to be spoken. The moral I want to impress upon you here is that alcoholics are MAJOR red flags! Dating one can only lead to heartache and pain (And as the Foreigner song goes, I don't know if I can face it again! I choose not to!).

If you've never dated an alcoholic, allow me to impart some wisdom. Drinking in bars can get expensive (especially for you gentlemen—three glasses of her wine is at least $27 before tax, tip and food), and people are watching (one of the reasons they enjoy bar hopping so much). I'd bet my next paycheck that Yugo privately sucked down at least one bottle of wine (the more often they drink, the more they need to reach the desired buzz) at home prior to our date in order to save money and face. It's what they do. No bueno.

Addicts are also notorious liars (and there's no gender bias to this) so don't think you're going to get an honest answer when you ask anything. They lie to themselves and then to everyone else. They're in denial of their problem, expertly finding excuses and other people to blame. Eliciting your sympathy (with their lies) is also big with them. It's all part of their survival mechanism. Keeping the sympathy and attention on themselves helps them justify their drinking, and thus their lies. "I drink to numb the pain" rather than dealing with their issues head on like a responsible, healthy adult. News flash — your problem(s) will still be there when you sober up! They say it makes them feel good, however, you cannot drink to feel better. Alcohol is a depressant, and alcoholism is a disease. Oh, it might feel good in the moment, but eventually you are going to get angry or weepy, sad or pukey, and ultimately hungover. Their "Poor Me!" routine keeps you loving them, often acting as their enabler. They will always find someone else to blame — usually the enabler — everything's all your fault! When you decide to stop (being abused) enabling, they'll find someone else to take over. It's a sad display but it works for them, all part and parcel of the disease — and they don't want to stop!

It's very hard to let go of a lover who is charming, smart, fun and attractive. Even more arduous if they are also funny, successful, etc. Triple threat if you desire to play hero/savior and caretaker, trying to heal/cure the inebriated (S/he NEEDS me!). You're not the hero, though — you're the enabler. While it may be tempting to try to tame the tippler, it's a longshot at best. Fight the urge and RUN! You cannot, I repeat, CANNOT change them! They enjoy the drink too much and you will never mean more to them than their liquid love.

I can empathically hear you thinking, "People can change! There's rehab!" I often used to fantasize about this for the one man I ever really loved (who later drank himself to death), but my dad said something that made a lot of sense. "If he rehabbed, he would no longer be the man you fell in love with. Accept that he can never be what you want him to be."

An addictive personality is hard to rehab. They trade one addiction for another. Move on, and don't look back!

Tanned Anorexic

This is another from the pre-computer days when photos were not available. You really had to trust when the person described himself as handsome. I think this clown actually described himself as extremely handsome. That's generally a turn-off for me. I don't want anyone *too* pretty, lest all the women hang on him and his big head can't fit through the door. Also, to boast this seems rather arrogant, eh!

I arrived at the designated place on time and spotted him immediately. Not sure if it was the glare from his uber white teeth, or the nuclear glow from his orange tan. We said our hellos and it was clear neither of us was attracted to the other. The venue was packed, Friday night, so we decided to move to a less popular place. He left before me, and I saw the white Cadillac he got into, so when I arrived at the new location and didn't see his car, I figured he'd blown me off and didn't bother parking. WOOHOO! Yes, I was elated. I'd wasted enough time driving to two different restaurants and dreaded having to make small talk with someone so immeasurably far from my wish list.

This one needs no explanation. Let him go — Blech!

Suckwind

I've met minimalists before, but this guy took the cake! Still in the early days of my learning curve, I agreed to meet Sucky at his place AND also did not get enough of his basic life story over the phone. Dumb dumb dumb!!

There are bells and whistles going off in my head when a seemingly active and otherwise healthy man tells me he's awaiting a disability retirement, having been struck over the back with a mop one time by an inmate while working as a prison guard. OK, I understand it's a dangerous job and people do get permanently injured (or hurt and unable to work temporarily), I just wasn't buying the full-blown disability in this case. Red flag for me.

He was an Asian Indian, said he'd cook authentic Indian food for me, and that sounded enticing enough. The first thing I noticed when I entered his place was the saturated scent of curry. But it wasn't just in the air and wall paper — it seemed to literally be seeping from his very pores! He smelled like hot garbage.

It can be awkward when a man cooks for me, if he thinks he is so good at it and is looking for that male ego stroking. I'm often left speechless — not just because I wish to remain polite, but because there's usually something really dry stuck in my throat. He did make chicken masala, and it tasted fine. But. He stood over me while I chewed, and rushed me so he could wash the plate! Dafuq? Hard to buy the disability thing the way he flew around the room. What's yer hurry, pal? I think he was so quer-

to get me upstairs (didn't own a couch)
'V'. On his musty mattress. With no bed
floor. Spared the sheets too. Prolly threw
laundry right before I got there so I

ck & white TV stood on a small bureau,
foil-wrapped antennas. I remember be-
getting up to change the channels, what
l. As Sucky lay there on his side trying to
d a courteous "sorry to chew and screw"
"Ooooh, look at the time... Gotta go!"

disabled, with not even a bed to his name,
uld he make? I was young, my whole life
ature would I have had with him? What
e as a mate? Methinks I would've been
nothing more than a convenience to him, whether for a night or a
lifetime. No thanks!

Sean of the Jungle

Seemed like a decent catch, and couldn't have come at a better time since I was just coming off a breakup with the only man I ever really loved, and wanted to move on quickly. We met out in his neck of the woods; long drive, but along the shore, nice way to spend a day. We had a great time over a fancy brunch and agreed to continue dating. Due to the distance involved, we didn't see much of each other, and it was clear to me he'd be dating others. That's not illegal, but ideally we'd be exclusive.

On our second date, he swung by a parking lot and 'happened to' run into a friend of his. So obvious. Like what are you, 15? The friend took a good look at me, nodded (his approval) at Sean, then they laughed and said their goodbyes. Minus two points for maturity (yes, we keep score!). Later that night, we'd ordered pizza delivery and I remember him asking for "everything 'cept sewer trout". (I hate anchovies too) I assume this was his usual since the counterperson didn't seem to question it. Cute, in an immature kinda way...

One rainy afternoon, he lit a romantic fire and set the mood. I knew it wouldn't be long before we'd become more intimate as it seemed like we were progressing nicely. I therefore cannot say I was surprised when he disappeared into the bedroom and came out soon after — wearing a leopard-print bikini! OK, I can appreciate what he was going for here, however, I burst out laughing just the same. He looked ridiculous! This was a turn-off!

He laughed too, praise be, and we kissed a bit. I could see he was excited. Then I watched in silent horror as he proceeded to pleasure himself. Yeah. I was young, had never seen this phenomenon before, and felt rather put off. He moaned his way toward orgasm as I looked away, and I recall thinking, "If you need me, I'll be over here..." When he was done soon after — and this is emblazoned in my mind forever — he casually said — in over-pronounced words as the empty lotion bottle exhaled its last blurps — "Hhhhhmmm, I'll have to get more co-coa but-ter!" No wonder his hands were eerily smooth, like *too* smooth! Ick!! I was more than a little creeped out.

Where's the door?!

I should have ended it right there, but I did what most single people coming off a breakup do — stay with whomever they are currently settling for so they don't have to be alone. This is a mistake, people! I understand the loneliness, and chances are the person you're biding time with feels the lack of intimacy but is doing the same — with either of you ready to jump ship if/when someone 'better' comes along.

I never actually saw him again, but not because of all that. The deal breaker came very soon after. He'd called a few days before Christmas and gave it the ol' "I'm not feeling too well <cough cough>. I'll call you after Christmas!"

Wow. How stoopid am I! He had mentioned his ex-girlfriend (whom he was still in love with) comes to town around the holidaze to be with her family. How nice of him to place me on the back burner — at Christmas! — until she returned to wherever she now lived. Sorry pal, Ali don't play dat! Buhbyyyye! And good riddance!

Ladies, if he's still stuck on someone else, you don't have a prayer! It doesn't matter how pretty you are, how smart, sexy, fun, rich, or talented/tolerant you are in bed — I'm convinced men only love this way once, and the chances of you winning him over are slim to none! You would just be the side piece while he holds the door open for her. If he even *mentions* the ex on the first date in a loving way, show yourself out! You deserve someone who's emotionally available. Leopard print optional.

This applies to you men as well, and includes the flipside — If s/he mentions the ex in a not-so-loving way, s/he's still got baggage s/he needs to work through and you don't need to be a sounding board for that noise. The moment a man starts talking about the ex, I envision excusing myself "to the ladies' room" — and walking right out the front door! Buh-bye! "No time left for you — on my way to better things! I found myself some wings!" Your time is precious. NEXT!!

Dr. Gene X

This guy was filthy rich, and very handsome. He had a Baby Grand in his mansion, and I happen to play a bit. Great catch, right? Wrong! He was still in love with his ex — a young woman with two kids who were not his, but whom he insisted on supporting despite the fact he'd likely never see any of them again. He said he'd rather they get the money than Uncle Sam. I'd say that's a noble thing if not for the fact that he would've dropped everything to get the woman back.

Again, you don't stand a chance if your date is still in love with someone else. This man lived in another state and was ready to send me a plane ticket so we could meet, but at the 12th hour he decided he was too much of an emotional mess to be anything to me. He'd occasionally message me afterward, or call me during a crying fit (TAXI!) to ask if I was happy. Clearly, he was not. I suspect he was suffering with depression and hated being alone, but it wasn't me he wanted to be with.

I want to be wanted. Be special to someone. Hold out for nothing less!

John the Rapist

This is not a good, funny story. And yet, it's an amazing one! For this reason, I felt it belonged here even though it doesn't necessarily flow with the humorous tone. I've actually written a separate piece on just this story. In fact, the tale is SO amazing that I wrote a screenplay about it. This one needed to be seen on the wide screen! Long story short, after pitching it over the phone, I sent the treatment to a major network's production company. They sent back a generic "Thanks but no thanks" letter, which I immediately circular filed… My ego was flattened; I wasn't thinking. No matter, if I chose to sue, I could subpoena phone records. Anyhoo, their movie was called She Cried No, starring Candice Cameron. My screenplay was called Renata. This was the name I chose for my alter ego femme fatale. For anyone about to rush to get a dictionary (do those things still exist?), I will save you the trouble. According to Dictionary.com, a femme fatale is an irresistibly attractive woman, especially one who leads men into disastrous situations. Renata was that for me—and thus him. Long story short, girl gets raped, serves up her own brand of justice, and creates a movie about it to expose the perp publicly. The production company, to which I heavily sold the idea to (you never hear anything on date rape!), decided it didn't fit their format. So they turned down my treatment, stole the premise and made it fit — college girl gets acquaintance raped, creates a video about it after campus police do nothing, exposes the boy and justice is served. Viola!

Rapist lived over an hour away. Of course I considered whether or not I wanted to start a long-distance relationship, but I've always said I'd rather have one Mr. Right an hour away than 10 not-so-rights close to home! Depending on where you live (A friend in CA used to drive eight hours to see her boyfriend in Arizona), an hour might not sound like much to you, but here in RI, where everything is only 20 minutes or less away, you consider packing a lunch or overnight bag for a one-hour drive! Lots of seemingly-great potential suiters dropped me because they didn't want to do the drive (but what if I'm worth it?! One of us can move eventually!).

Anyhoo, Rapist had a larger plan which I didn't see while experiencing each part of its baby steps. His agenda was this. He would call me a few nights per week for two weeks, too busy to meet but thoroughly expressing interest. In doing so, he earned my trust quickly. Having this trust, he insisted on 'being the gentleman' and picking me up at my door for our date (Picture flowers in hand. But no, that didn't happen). Mistake number one, giving him my address. He was still a stranger, no matter how comfortable I felt with him. I was already smitten, and he knew it. Mistake number two, agreeing to let him drive. You'll see why in a bit.

Our big date was to be dinner on the Cape. I was so excited! Well, Cape Cod is a big place, and it was about two hours from my home. John had already driven over an hour before getting to my door. He'd arrived late, and when I opened the door... Blech! Wiry comb-over, wiry lips, big bad wolf teeth. I was NOT attracted at all! (Remember, no pictures in the early days of ads) Despite my pleas (I was so ready to bail, but he'd driven all that way), he still insisted our date was to be on the Cape — and not just anywhere, but aaaall the way to the tip of Provincetown! I protested that it was a Sunday night, I had work in the morning and we should just stay local, but no, this was "going to be the best date ever!"

Along the way, despite the time, he insisted on stopping at Dairy Queen. "Dessert first!" (Best. Date. Ever) We had our Blizzards and were on our way. We miraculously found a place for dinner in Truro; most establishments had stopped serving at 11pm. He ordered for me and spread the brie on my bread, ever the romantic gentleman. Never mind my growing dis-ease over the fact that it was getting so late. Instead of heading south toward home, he went north toward Ptown! Great. He said there was a *fabulous* parade I just had to see! By the time we arrived it was 2am, yet this parade was in full swing. For those who don't know, Ptown is the Mecca for gay men. Not that there's anything wrong with that, but I, as a hetero woman, was not pleased watching my date happily skipping down the road alongside the guys in the tutus. Yeah. Never mind red flag waving — this was a tapestry blowing furiously!

He was surely ("Don't call me Shirley!") bi, definitely not gay. Come 3am, I suggested we get home, but he insisted otherwise. "Wouldn't it be romantic to wake up by the shore? Don't you ever do anything spontaneous? Live a little!" He said he was too tired to drive; I said I would. He said that's the man's job… In the end, I was painted into a corner and there was nowhere to run, no one to scream to. Perfect date? More like the perfect date rape.

For many years, I blamed myself. That's what rape victims do. I told myself it was my fault because I wasn't a stoopid woman, yet I'd put myself in a position where he could so easily take advantage of me. Oh yeah, he had this down — right down to the locations and times. In retrospect, he'd planned this whole night waaaay ahead of time. So well, in fact, that I was convinced he'd done this before — to many woman — and I was determined to prove it.

Best. Date. Ever. I thought about some of the things he'd done: arriving late, insisting on stopping for a dessert that would further delay us so we'd be at the Cape late, far from home at 4am, having me make a playful call to his work voicemail so it would appear we weren't even together if I later cried rape. He'd covered his tracks in many ways, so it really was a near-perfect crime. Well played, Mr. Rapist, but I'm smarter.

Rape is hard enough for victims to talk about. Call it morbid curiosity; everyone wants to hear the sordid details, but it's really none of your business. It took ten years before I myself was able to talk about it. Without giving away too much information — after all, I just may make this story my next book — I will tell you that I set in motion a plan so simple yet so successful, I felt like Mr. Magoo after totally taking him down by accident! Because he was a part-time police officer, and because so much time had gone by when I finally admitted to myself this was rape, I didn't feel comfortable reporting it. Instead, I took justice vigilante style. He of all people would have to agree, special times call for special measures, eh! Sometimes you just have to take matters into your own hands. That's exactly what I did.

My initial goal was beyond simplistic. Never could I have imagined the plot would thicken, and be so successful because of his sheer hubris and insane desire to control things. Looooong story short, I wreaked havoc in his life, basically with his permission! After planting a bogus ad and watching him take the bait, I incited fear, cost him money, and mebbe even his job. In his crazy need to meet this woman who didn't exist (so he could play his game on her too), he chased "me" for six months! Eventually, I got really tired of the whole thing. I'd done my part and was no longer curious to see just how long he'd stoopidly chase Renata. We want what we can't have, and he just couldn't get to her!

Please understand, I am not typically a vengeful person and was not enjoying this. I saw an opportunity and knew I had to complete my mission for the greater good. I felt it was somehow my duty to shut him down. Many times I tried to end the mission, as it took a toll on me emotionally, but his actions — utter haughtiness — begged me to keep stringing him along. I really wish I could share this moment with you now in more detail, but it needs to be told another way, another time.

The story was so awesome (Network of friends spanning four states were happy to help!) that I just had to create a movie about it! My end goal was to have produced a true-to-life film that he might one day bring his date to. Picture him sitting there in the theater with his (next victim) unsuspecting lady, hole in the popcorn bucket, watching his MO unfold before him on the wide screen! His date might even catch on, or better yet, all the women who were his victims prior! How kewl would that be?! While I was pleasantly successful in taking him down a notch, I was not successful with the film. As you know, the screenplay was robbed, and it felt like I'd been raped all over again! However, I was not willing to take on a lengthy legal battle with a major giant.

Soon after, I went to a well-known psychic. Yes, I believe, but I don't believe everyone with a sign on the sidewalk reading 'gifted and talented psychic' is good at what s/he does. I've been to many, and this woman Virginia, rest her soul, was one of the very few who could ever read me. She told me of past events, saw my daughter preconception, and she saw *him*. With a confused look on her face, she asked me, "Did you date a cop?" My cousin Lora was whacking me under the table — this had to be him! Virginia then said, "I don't know what it is, but because of you — something you did — this man is no longer abusing women."

HUZZAH!! Yeah. I did that. I'm here to help. ☺

I later did some research and learned a lot about rape. Most women don't think, or aren't sure, that what happened to them was officially rape. They may blame themselves, or call it some lesser form of molestation, too ashamed to come forward and invite the long legal process into their lives once they do come to accept. It's easier to bury it and (try to) move on. Varying state to state, the statute of limitations ranges from three years to 30. It often takes many years before you feel strong enough to come forward, and it's usually therapeutic, despite the madness of court, after so many years of holding it in. It may be hard to prove, but the law has to listen. Gone are the days of dragging a victim through the mud in order to get the rapist freed. Rest assured, you don't have to be a church goer to expose a rapist. You're doing a public service. Be proud of that. Finally, get help if need be. There's no shame in it!

Rape and molestation are a helluva lot more common than you may think! The last statistics I saw were staggering. What makes date rape a different breed is that you weren't jogging down the road and shoved into the bushes — you accepted a date with someone you thought you knew and trusted! That messes with your mind as much as your body. People tend to tone down date rape as though it's not as severe as 'regular' rape, but it's just as real and just as emotionally painful.

So many morals to this one. Always trust your instincts (Fight or flight — RUN when that inner voice tells you to!). Choose wisely if the person you are chatting with lives considerably far away. Be very selective before you give out your phone number, and even more choosey when you agree to meet! When that time comes, meet at a public place. Have your own transportation, and make sure you have emergency cash on hand (in case credit is not an option). Tell a friend where you are going, with whom, and provide that person's contact information (My friends knew I would leave a sticky note on my fridge, so there could be no miscommunication if I disappeared, and no needlessly worrying anyone every time I had a date). These are the rules! I follow them a lot more closely because of this experience. Live and learn.

If you feel scared — you should! Trust that gut feeling! The world can be a scary place. Be prepared! FOLLOW THE RULES!!

Mr. Clean

He sure seemed normal. Nice voice, intelligent, easy to talk to. I won't say he was a loquacious fellow, as I found myself having to carry the conversation. This is a constant problem, however, and I like to think the man will come out of his shell as he feels more comfortable with me. About twenty minutes into the conversation, he told me he'd like to clean my house for me, half naked.

I was never really clear on which half was to be naked, or which one of us that referred to, but I had a fairly good idea. I told him this was a little too freaky for me and wished him well.

Then I kicked myself! A good-looking, buff guy wanted to strip down and clean my house for me — for free! And I said NO! Ugh!! How stoopid can one woman be?!

We all know, though, that this could not have ended well, and of course I made the wisest decision.

There are all kinds of fetishes out there I never knew existed, but after talking to some of these online men, I've become more enlightened.

Mr. Clean called me about two months later, as if no time had passed and no dysfunction existed. I said I was busy.

Mister Minister

This guy was a blonde, preppy minister looking for a wife —
SO not my type! But there was nobody else banging my door
down, and I was lonely, figured What the hey. We met for coffee
and had a nice conversation. At one point he said to me, clear out
of the blue, "Everyone knows someone who's had an abortion,
whether they know it or not." I asked him to repeat that, as it was
so profound, so true, and... Dafuq? Why was he telling me this?!

We later said our goodbyes, and I think we both knew
there'd be no 'next time'. As I drove home, pondering the words
he'd laid on me, it hit me like a ton of bricks — We'd met before!
Clearly, Mister Minister remembered *me* right away.

It was a few years earlier, before my marriage/divorce,
when I was living with my now-late father. I had come home from
college classes for the day. When I walked through the door, this
man was seated at the table. My dad was standing against the
wall. They greeted me and invited me to join their conversation.
I dutifully did as told; Dad introduced me to Reverend X. I was
extremely uncomfortable, 40,000 things I'd rather be doing in
that moment.

After a few pleasantries, Dad blurted, "Abortion is wrong,
but adoption is a beautiful thing!" Okay, great! I was so weirded
out, I just agreed, stood up and excused myself so *they* could talk.
This was not my guest, nor my idea of High Tea. I didn't understand at the time, but this was an intervention! Dad had invited

this minister over specifically to talk to me in case I ever got pregnant so that I wouldn't abort. What impression does this leave on the man making the trip over to talk to the girl though?!

My Protestant father had brought this clergyman in to talk to me because he didn't know how to broach the subject himself. He'd always said, "Don't come home pregnant!" and maybe he thought I would leave or do something drastic rather than confide in him. I will never know; this is all speculation and the pieces seem to fit. The good reverend, then, was trying to tip me off as to how we'd met. He likely believed I'd had an abortion, and was either letting me know he wasn't judging me, or letting me know I wasn't wifey material for him. Or both. Either way, we were not a match. I like to think it was one of those reason/season/lifetime learning opportunities. Next!

If there's a lesson here, it's just one more in a long line of "This state is too small!" More than once I've run into people whom I'd either met before, or knew of me through a mutual friend. You never know what they've heard about you, what preconceived notions are in place. Just know that if this happens, roll with it as there's not much you can do to change it. First impressions are just that, and you had yours already — whether you know it or not.

Mr. Character Actor

He is thusly named since this is how he described his looks when we spoke over the phone prior to meeting. I wasn't sure what to expect, but when I met him, I knew instantly. He would never be the lead actor because he was, quite simply, rather fugly. We're talking weathered skin, huge droopy ears, no eyebrows, very long in the teeth. Carrying on a conversation seemed to be a problem for him, so I had to carry it, which never fails to turn me off. Have you no social skills?! This is why, when the tab came and he said, "Your half of the bill is…," I was immediately put off. I understand times have changed; a woman cannot automatically expect the male to pick up the tab (but extra points if he does! See Plenty of Toads). It's a respectful gesture from a gentleman when he does offer, especially if he wishes to court the lady further. That, and my entertainment doesn't come free! Sheesh! I could've stayed home alone and had more fun! I put my money down, walked him out and couldn't leave fast enough.

As the valets were letting us into our respective cars, I heard my Oscar loser yell over, "OK, see you soon!" What a character! I ignored this and got into my car. The valet looked at me questioningly and said, "Your boyfriend is trying to tell you something!" I just winked at the boy — and drove off very quickly. I then looked over at ol' Dumbo, who was still waving furiously, telling me to have a good night. (Don't tell me what to do!)

Nothing screams ad date like having the guy yell, "Nice meeting you!" across the parking lot. Ugh.

In retrospect, I hadn't spent enough time on the phone with this man prior to our meeting. If I had, I would've realized he could not converse beyond the weather update. I'm not saying spend weeks on the phone. I'm saying see if you can really talk for at least ten minutes (but no more than 20 unless you're really hitting it off). Looks fade, people. Think quality of life. When you're 90 and sitting at the breakfast table, you want to be sitting across from someone who is able to hold a conversation. You can silently stare into your grapefruit for just so long before nodding off. Choosing a younger partner isn't a guarantee of that quality either. You'll still be watching your partner stare at the prune juice, the silence deafening.

Ivan the Terrible

This guy was very pretty, had some cosmetic surgery after getting his nose broken in a fight (That's what happens when you used to break legs for a living). Apparently he wasn't so terrible in the sack. He had told me a story about how, while standing in line with his (now ex) wife in the grocery store, a woman he'd slept with yeeeears before on the other side of the country (where he was admittedly a womanizer) recognized him (like what are the chances?!), turned to his wife and said, "Your husband is an ass----!" Ivanho himself fully admits he is, or was (but still is) an arrogant ass----.

I asked how his wife handled it. Apparently, she was taken by surprise and said nothing.

Ever the comedian, I think I would've handled it differently if that angry woman in line were addressing *me* about this!
Her: Your husband is an ass----!
Me: Well, you can't have it both ways, can you?
Her: Huh?
Me: Well didn't he rock your world? A guy doesn't become *that* amazing in bed by being a GOOD boy!

Yup, women love the bad boys. It's an inherent Darwinian thing, choosing the strongest male to sire our children. It can't be fought easily, but rather, only after we've taken several kicks to the head by bad boys who broke our heart. Eventually, we grow to realize what really matters, and lean toward the dependable, considerate guys to spend our twilight years with. (Conversely, most guys want the trophy wives, and I'm not convinced they ever outgrow that) We want what we want, though, and hope to have it all! I often fantasize about building a Fly Machine (think Geoffrey Goldblum). I'd throw in the handsome buff guy, the amazing lover, the brilliant conversationalist and the loyal care-taker. I'd flick the switch, and out would walk the perfect husband (Sorry ladies, the machine gets destroyed once my man walks out!).

But I digress. We all know the bad boy stereotype, right, ladies? Hey, we're all adults here — If you're only looking for a booty call, just say so! It saves everyone the hassle of lying, and believing the hurtful lies. There are plenty of depraved people out there willing to take you on.

After a cheapo dinner at a large chain restaurant with his 10-yr-old son in tow (DON'T DO THIS! LEAVE THE KIDS OUT OF IT!), we dropped off the kid at his ex's house (this is when the intelligent conversation ended. Loved the kid!) and went back to his place where he (made me take off my shoes and) liter-ally took me by the hand to his upstairs bedroom. I could've ar-gued here, said that I never do this sort of thing (what every woman says right before a one-night stand) or admitted to not having been with a man for over 12 years (TRUTH!) but what was the use? He'd never believe it anyway. Women say, "This isn't something I normally do," or even, "I've never done this be-fore!" The men expect this lie and ignore it. I was giving in and he knew it.

I'm often torn between being the good Catholic girl I was raised to be, and being a normal, libido-healthy consenting adult in the 21st century. There was a time I would have chosen the prude route, but at this point, I am a middle-aged recovering Catholic woman still in my prime. Ain't nobody throwin' himself at me these days, so when a gorgeous bodybuilder with lead actor looks makes the offer, who am I to decline?! No one can use you without your permission, and this guy had my blessing. Not a very safe thing to do — at all. What can I say, I'm human too. Walk tall and carry condoms.

There's an unspoken rule that if you sleep with a guy on the first date, he ain't callin' again. I told myself we'd both want to know if the other was worth the long drive if this was to continue, but we both knew he wasn't calling again — despite his attempts to pretend otherwise. All part of the game.

Afterward, he told me I could stay overnight, but the caveat was that I had to be out by 5am, citing a daytrip with his son in the early morning. The *carrot* was that next time he'd come to *my* place (a two-hour drive. He's no fool! You don't $h!t where you eat!).

I was so sure he wasn't going to come the following Saturday — my birthday — that I had already posted a pic on Facebook of myself with friends celebrating my special day out in Newport — just minutes before he texted me to say his son was sick and he couldn't make it after all, so sorry! (Duh!) He even commented on my Newport photo! "Wish I could be there!" Uh huh. Yeah... His son got sick a lot, apparently (and if it's your birthday, the cheapos will run). Not wanting to be back-burner fodder for him, I eventually blew him off by 'unfriending' him on Facebook. *POOF!* Not one to be rejected, and trying not to look like the ass----, he soon found me on LinkedIn and sent a friendly hello. Bait is cheap.

It's not a good idea to become friends on Facebook (or other social media) with someone you're potentially dating at first since they get to see what you're up to, who your family and friends are, personal info, etc. Some strangers become scary stalker types! And with no privacy on either end, you may not like what you see. Before 'unfriending' Ivanho, I noticed an exchange between him and a woman on his FB wall soon after our Newport blunder. She was shamelessly throwing herself at him (Forget that, ladies! Men love the chase! If you are too easy to get, they will look elsewhere!), trying to pin him down for a munch date*. It took amazing fortitude avoiding the temptation to post my own comment on their exchange, "Susan — Gotta be out by 5am! Unfortunately for her, his son was sick.

*While writing this snippet, I accidentally typed M instead of L for lunch and the word came out munch. HAHA, munch date—It was so incredibly perfect, exactly what I was going for there, I absotively had to keep it in! I'm sure I've never heard it before. I expect this term to totally take off, and want full credit for coining it!!

Wally Peepers

I had taken a break from online dating, and decided to give it another go. The first man to respond was not a looker, but a seemingly decent, hard-working single father of one son. What harm could a meeting do? Calling this one Wally Peepers because of the thickness of his glasses. Eyewear has made great strides over the last several years, so if he is still wearing the proverbial Coke-bottle glasses, I'm thinking he hasn't splurged on himself since the 80s. For a man who makes decent money, this can tell you a few things about him. Is he cheap? Just doesn't care about fashion in the least, or his appearance? Does he get to a doctor regularly?

As mentioned, I find it's usually best to meet over coffee. That way, if things aren't going well, you can excuse yourself quickly and salvage the rest of your day. I was surprised when this man suggested a movie for our first meeting, as it's not the sort of place where you can converse easily.

However, there is the flip side to consider, especially if the guy seems a bit dull. You can learn a lot from a person by going to the movies! Did he bitch about the price of the ticket? Did he offer to buy popcorn or a drink, even if you just ate? Does he whine, and find fault with everything during the movie? Does he try to hold your hand? Does he hold your arm while walking in/out? Did he talk your ear off at high volume throughout? Did he turn his phone off? These are all things that can tell you much about a person!

I met him there, we sat and then the show began… It was a bitter cold winter day, the theater was apparently conserving resources and my hands were freezing, so I kept my gloves on. Halfway through the movie, my date commented, "Why don't you do some exercise? Then you'd have some blood flow!" GRRRRRRRRRRR!! It may not look it, but I'm no sofa spud! I do cardio kickboxing two days a week, Pilates two nights a week, treadmill or spin bike, yoga, and hike at least three times per week. I can run circles around skinny women half my age, and instantly grew silent when hearing this dig. Looking at him, I think I drew blood on my tongue while trying to hold back what I was thinking — "When's the last time you did a sit-up or lifted so much as a phone book!?!"

At the end of the movie, he made the comment, "It was really stupid of you to suggest seeing a movie on the first date. We couldn't talk, the movie was too long and it sucked. Our next date should be something simple."

Um, next date?? I wished him a nice life, and walked off into the sunset.

Meet for a 10-minute cup of coffee, trust your instincts, run when the red flag starts waving!

Unbecoming Officer

This man lived an hour and a half away, which, as you know, is a big deal to us Rhode Islanders. He seemed great, though, so I looked forward to meeting him. He'd described his body type as barrel-chested. He was a barrel alright — all belly. Against my better judgment, I agreed to see a movie for our first date (seriously, what's the point if you can't converse?!). The conversation before the movie went well. He was actually very interesting, had some war tales from Desert Storm. While a good soldier never tells the gory details, I was married to a Special Forces Army vet and could fill in the gaps.

He'd also told me about how he'd lost his front teeth — not in the war, but while preparing for a blind date! He said he was under his car doing some repairs when the lift let go, trapping him underneath. Right about that time, his date appeared. Apparently, she was so freaked out by the horrific sight, she ran! (Call yer own damn ambulance!) And that, as they say, was that.

Right before the movie started, he turned to me — and shoved his tongue down my throat rather aggressively. Totally taken aback, I pulled away and asked what that was about. He said he didn't know, just got overwhelmed with passion because he (hadn't been with a woman in forever?) was so attracted to me. Awkward! We watched the war movie without further incident. At the end of the evening, he asked if I thought we should pursue this. Not sharing his passion, I merely smiled. He took the hint. Back to the drawing board...

♥

Methinks all this could've been avoided if I'd made my 10-minute coffee rule sooner, but sometimes ya need a few kicks to the head before ya learn.

You don't know how it feels...
To be meeee!

Country Cole

This guy lived in Tennessee, far from my home and mentality. Don't southerners hate us damn Yankees? (Oh wait — Up north I guess we're just Yankees. It's when we move down there that we become *Damn* Yankees! Has anyone ever told them 'Yankee' means nothing to us? The war is over, you lost, get over it!) I'm not really sure why Cole chose to select a Yank 4,000 miles away, but he was cute and I wasn't especially tied down anywhere, so I gave it a chance.

Like most others, he seemed very decent on the phone and I looked forward to meeting him. Coffee would be a bit of a challenge this time though. Luckily, he was a successful businessman and southern gentleman — He supplied a plane ticket for me to come visit.

Less than a week before my departure, he called to say he had a skin rash and had to postpone my visit. Not cancel — postpone — and he offered to fax me the doctor's note if I didn't believe him. I declined the offer, however, my spider sense was tingling. Whether he had something on his skin or something up his arse, he definitely had something up his sleeve. I patiently waited for him to choose the date of our next attempt at meeting, and rearranged my work schedule once again, but I knew enough to be prepared for anything.

He chose the week before Christmas. I thought this was sweet, as we could meet around Christmas and share the holiday, but be with our loved-ones for the actual day. Sure enough, about a week before we were to meet, he again called to say something had come up. I challenged him to give it to me straight — Why was he putting off our meeting — again?! I could tell he had been drinking (red flag waving!!). He said he was having a Christmas party for his employees the week I'd be there, and he didn't feel comfortable bringing me, in case we didn't hit it off. I told him no problem, I'd just go exploring the area on my own the night of his party, but he said that would be wrong. As I pressed further, he admitted that, if things didn't work out, he'd be back to having no one and didn't want that. So, I was just to be a text buddy? Let's pretend we're in love with someone we've never met?

OK, that can happen, I admit I've felt the butterflies, but look what happened each and every time! I got my hopes raised, put the guy way up on a pedestal, only to find out he wasn't quite the god I'd built him up to be. In fact, sometimes I'd get to feeling like I wasn't good enough for said god, and I'd tell him my faults so he could decide if I was worthy. Don't you dare!! You are the queen, you are so worthy, and you don't know what you're getting until you meet and spend major quality time with a person.

As for my perfidious buddy Cole, he fell asleep while whining about his fears. I was kind enough to hang up so he wouldn't be charged for the long-distance call.

Country Cole might could use a clue. I thank him for the clues he sent prior to me getting on a plane. That could've been a complete disaster — the risk you take when starting something long distance. Of course he asked for the plane ticket back, but I felt I'd earned it. You don't get to yank my chain without recompense!

Mr. I Bought You Lunch, So . . .

He didn't look anything like his photos, but not so terrible I couldn't keep lunch down. After some boring conversation, he asked me to drive him to his car. Oh yeah, you just know where this is going. They try to get you into their car for some smooching, which they hope will lead to spoodydooting! When he asked me if he could kiss me, I just laughed! I couldn't help it, I'd been *here* so many times before! When I stopped laughing, he invited me to his house, "Just down the road!"

I responded with, "My dad always said, 'You can't blame a guy for trying!' So, nice try, but NO."

He responded with, "But I bought you lunch!"

♥

Wow. 'Nuff said?

donut

The lower-case spelling of his name is intentional. I don't even remember conversing with this guy prior to our first meeting, I only recall we met at a decent restaurant and conversed well enough over dinner. I do remember thinking, as he balled up his straw wrapper and started playing hockey across the table with it like a five-year-old, "Nice guy, just not for me." (RED FLAG WAVING!!) When we got back to my place (DUMB MOVE letting him pick me up in his car at my house!), he asked if he could kiss me goodbye. Like an idiot, I felt bad and said, "OK, but just a quick one!" You know how Bobby Brady saw fireworks when he kissed Millicent? That really can happen! I didn't understand it, but I didn't dismiss it either.

I knew we had precious little in common, but we were both lonely and bored at the time. In fact, he was still in love with his ex-girlfriend. After ten years of dating him, at 20 years his senior (she was his mother's best friend. Yeah.), she left him for someone ten years younger than him! Thing is, it seemed like she only took her underwear when she left their apartment — everything else was still there, like she was coming home any day! He seemed to like that arrangement, and because I wasn't even remotely in like, never mind love, I just didn't care. Several months later, I was pregnant with our daughter. Yeah. It was not the plan, but I'm sorta stuck with him for life now.

I affectionately call him donut to this day (behind his back). At the time, I was an editor for the USPS, and worked with several communications specialists throughout the New England district. A teleconference call with my Maine correspondent had a poor connection, and when she heard me refer to the baby daddy as 'The Donor' (he initially wanted nothing to do with the baby), she thought I was saying donut. It took me all of five seconds to adopt this name, saying, "You know, it's truly fitting! Useless, hole in the head… Yeah, I LIKE IT!" The name has stuck ever since (SHhhhhhhh, don't tell him! I kept it a secret from my daughter for 15 years until Davey Downer let the cat out of the bag, UGH! More on Davey Downer later).

Being pregnant, and raising a child alone had me nearly dateless for over fourteen years. I then met up with an old friend from high school; we gave it a whirl for three months, but it didn't last. (The dreaded three-month mark!*) After that, I got the fever and wanted a man in my life, so I started the online dating thing again. As for donut, in case you were wondering, the old boy married someone a year after our breakup whom he'd also met online. I'd say some people have all the luck, but just because you're content in your rut doesn't mean you're truly happy. I do, however, know several people who married others they'd met online, and they are very happy, so I kept the faith!

Not sure what the moral is here. Use protection? In my defense, I did buy condoms, but because his (only) previous girlfriend was post-menopausal, they never had to worry about birth control, so I didn't know that he didn't know how to use a condom… Looking at the bigger picture, I knew upfront that he wasn't for me but continued to start a relationship anyway. I didn't trust my instincts, even though they were blaring! Blaring past the skyrockets! I know it's tough feeling lonely. It's nice having someone to do fun things with, but it's really unfair to have a relationship with someone just until something better comes along. Wait it out. My daughter was meant to be, so I can't say I totally regret having had this relationship, but it was never ever going to last (And, sadly, this is nearly the only ad person I've actually gotten past a second date with! <sigh>).

* Statistically speaking, around the three-month mark, we tend to let down our guard, stop being more polite than we really are, and let our true colors show. Relationships tend to get tested, and this is generally the point where you know whether it's going to last, or needs to end. I'm not wrong — it's a thing! Most new relationships end here — a season — if they're not meant to last awhile.

Alison O'Donnell

Mr. Adopted

I can't say this meeting went well. I had to bring my daughter, who was only four at the time, which he didn't seem to mind. He said he understood because he was adopted... and couldn't seem to let that topic drop. Not sure why some adopted folks feel the need to put that info out there. I assume this is more for their sake than ours. Mayhap, a way of dealing with abandonment issues? Even friends who've come from very wonderful, loving adoptive families have mentioned they were adopted, and are usually curious about their origin, even looking for their natural parents. It's normal to want to know where you came from; I respect this greatly. I just think mebbe it's not necessary info on a first meeting.

We met for lunch and he gladly paid. Boasted about how successful he is, and how generous he is with strangers, having set up a single mom/bartender with weekly funds to help pay for her night school. (Beware the braggarts!)

The jury in my mind was still out on this one when a fly whizzed by (Goldblum?), relentlessly buzzing around my head as we ate. Beyond annoyed, I quickly reached out, effortlessly caught the little bugger in mid-air, and lightly slammed it down onto the table in one fell swoop.

Another man might have appreciated my ninja-like prowess. Alas, his gape-mouthed wide-eyed silent stare strongly suggested I wouldn't be hearing from this one again. I was fine with

70

that. He had described himself as barrel-chested and fit; more like wobbling, swollen cask. Somewhere, a child is weeping.

Note to self: It's prolly wise to always put your best foot forward with a new date. First impressions are forever. It can be hard — I gotta be me! They'll find out who you are eventually, but mebbe on a first date you should do your best to get to the second? Yes, absotively be yourself and let your personality show through. However, in the immortal words of Austin Powers, "Oh, behave, baby!"

Denti Con Carne

We met up at the same sports bar I'd been using for these dates (waitress caught on to me!) and ordered chicken wings. The conversation was pleasant enough. We had some laughs, and when the date ended I agreed to a second one. I figured he must have partials as some teeth were too perfect next to the others, and his gut did not match his buff photos (he was balder too) but I pushed all that aside because I'm not perfect either. I felt he was a decent person, an improvement over everyone else I'd been meeting. My heart really wasn't in it, though, so it kinda sank when he asked if he could kiss me goodbye. (I refer you back to donut) I gave it the ol' archetypal "OK, but no tongue!!"

I call him Denti Con Carne here because, when he kissed me goodbye, slipping me the tongue (GRRRRR!), his dentures slipped too — and he deposited a piece of meat at the back of my mouth. Yeah. I just now puked a little in my mouth evoking this memory. As my friend Erin would say, "I can't get with that!" Second date cancelled.

Actually, I had intended to keep my word, and might have still gone through with the second date. However, he kept calling and asking, "Are you sure??... Are you sure, because if you're not..." Turn-off! Now very sure, I said, "Perhaps you're right, we prolly should not have a second date. <Sayonara!> Good luck!"

Confidence is sexy. A lack of confidence is a red flag.

Tooth Decay

Nice guy, very handsome, breath smelled like death. NEXT!

Halitosis can occur from either poor hygiene, rotting teeth, or an odd diet (and lack thereof; ketosis stage of dieting, better known as starvation). None of these bode well; bad breath (not the temporary kind, like coffee breath) is generally a red flag — a sure sign of poor health, no matter how temporary. If it smells like death, it prolly is. There's no mistaking the scent of rotting teeth. Unless he tells you he's getting a full set of dentures next week, you can bet you won't want to kiss him anytime soon.

Here's the thing about teeth. Call me shallow, but I have all mine and I don't think it's a lot to ask that my date have his. Things happen, I get it (see Unbecoming Officer!). Generally speaking, though, if you lose your teeth before it's age-appropriate to do so, it can be a red flag indicative of several things. Did this person drink/smoke too much at one time? Poor nutrition? Bar fights?? My dad brought me to the dentist twice a year for cleanings and checkups when I was a kid; his teeth were bad and he wanted me to have better. I take care of myself, and don't think it's a lot to ask that my date does as well. Survival of the fittest! And if you're missing a tooth, why haven't you replaced that bad boy yet?! If you're under 75 and still a viable date, it's well worth the investment.

I know it can be expensive, but there are ways. We always find a way when we want what we want, eh! Almost all dentists offer payment plans with a financer, but you may get a better rate if you shop around yourself first. You're hoping to meet someone special, why not put your best face forward? Get that tooth replaced! Of course you can still find love with someone who isn't shallow, but chances are s/he also is missing something. Just sayin'.

As famed advice columnist Ann Landers used to say, "It's all in the packaging!" How you market yourself — your appearance — can dictate who you are 'worthy' of. I struggle with my weight. It doesn't mean I'm unfit, as I know I'm strong and can run circles around the skinny-a$$ed wenches who have no trouble finding men, but it is what it is. I also despise makeup, even though I know I look so much better with it on. I will never be thin, and just have to trust that my man appreciates an au naturel woman with curves. However, I know enough to dress appropriately, comb my hair and brush my teeth (all of them!). Packaging.

Tewksbury fish

Still in the early days of making mistakes, I did the drive to this guy's apartment so we could go to dinner in my car (He didn't have one. I didn't know about the Three Tions back then. See page 133) 'Dinner out' turned out to be dinner in… Instead of saying he (is cheap) didn't have money to treat me for driving, he said he could give me a better meal without the expense. That's when he took two frozen Weight Watchers fish dinners out of the microwave. Gag! It was terribly dry. I don't even like fish! Not that he asked.

After the gagfest at the table, we moved to his couch. Immediately he moved in to kiss me — my cue to leave!

About two years later, I was chatting on the phone with a man and this story came up. As I started to tell him what happened that night, he got quiet, then asked me a few questions like, What was so wrong with frozen dinners? What was so wrong with the desire to kiss?… IT WAS HIM!

Clearly, this guy didn't make it into my cell phone because I didn't own one back then. Gotta love technology! Assuming he had the same phone number two years later, I would've known right away it was the same person when his name popped up. No shock that he was still single. Hopefully, he learned a lesson about frozen dinners being a no-no when wooing a woman, geesh!

Beantown Bonehead

"I didn't see anyone who looked like you," he said after I'd confronted him later. Nice. I drove all the way to Boston for that one, and paid big bucks for parking, only to get blown off! Doesn't sound like much to someone in a larger state who commutes two hours to work into a big city, but remember — here in RI, if you're not where you need to be in 20 minutes or less, you might as well pack a lunch or book a room! I like to think I'm not so small-minded. I'd much rather have a dollar than 100 pennies, so if I have to drive to get to the perfect man, so be it. This clearly was not him. On the bright side, I had a Saturday night in Boston, did some shopping, grabbed some food at the famed Faneuil Hall, and saw an awesome street act called The Human Knot (Australian funny man who juggles machetes and a chain saw atop a ladder. Find him on Instagram!).

This is a good place to point out that online dating can be a real blow to the ego sometimes. You feel awful when someone you'd gotten your hopes up about turns out to be something completely different. Back to the drawing board! Even worse is when the person skips out because he doesn't like what he sees (Sorry ladies, men are very visual creatures by nature, and most tend to make a snap judgment on your worthiness based on first impression appearance. If you don't immediately look doable in their eyes, they're gone!). I thought this guy was a gentleman because he had said he'd treat me to dinner and reimburse me for parking if I did the drive. I texted him on the long ride home, in response to his reply above, "That was low. After I traveled and paid for parking, the least you could've done was say 'Not interested'!" Cowards abound.

People are generally inauthentic. As humans, anything goes, from little white lies intended to make people feel better, to dating games and beyond. You conform to the job you're applying for at a job interview, and you make yourself out to be the perfect man/woman in a dating profile. You're selling yourself in an ad, so why wouldn't you make yourself sound great? The cowardice thing, however, doesn't fly with me. As a recovering Catholic, and the daughter of a brutally honest US Marine father, I have a big problem with dishonesty. And you can bet most people who make it a point to put 'honest' in their profile are liars.

Ironically, BB came back about a year later, having forgotten we'd conversed (My photos were updated). I kept the conversation going just to see where it would lead, get a feel for how he operates. No major spider sense tingling — until he invited me to Boston to meet for a drink. Geesh, not even parking fare this time?! Good-BYE!

Funny Boy

This guy was funny. And cute. We had lots of laughs over the phone for a week or two, and he made it seem like he was soooo into me, too. Oh, I really, really liked him! He called every day and made me laugh, and I just couldn't wait to meet him! One night, he started telling me about an episode of Walking Dead. He knew I was a fan and asked if I remembered the scene in the first season where a woman riding a bike had been cut in two and kept crawling. I immediately fell into a fit of laughter because I got the visual. The way he told it really cracked me up! Alas, he pulled a Houdini at that moment. "OK, I'm taking my daughter out for lobsters and have to take this call. (Huh? I didn't hear any...) It was nice talking to you!" Never heard from him again. Mebbe he hated my cute laugh. Mebbe he died from tainted shellfish.

OK, mebbe he bailed because I was laughing and not talking, but still I thought he was just too funny and I'd definitely hear from him again. After all, our call was cut short by his daughter, who takes priority over me... Right? (Note: people lie!) When he didn't call again, I was very disappointed. Not wanting to seem desperate, I did not attempt to reach him either; I very rarely chase these disappearing acts. IF SOMEONE IS INTERESTED, YOU WILL KNOW IT! However, I let some time go by and could see that his ad was still active, so at that point I took a chance and texted him. "Was it my maniacal laughter?" I asked. He did not respond.

Months later, I "accidentally" texted him. Bait is cheap, I know, but I really liked him and wanted to give him an "in" just in case his next woman didn't work out and he wanted to again explore things with me. I got the idea when I was writing a text to my daughter, "If you do that I'll have to eat all your pizza," and accidentally grabbed his name from the contacts, as it was right below my daughter's in the phone list. So, screw it, mebbe this was kismet! I hit send, then waited...

He didn't take the bait. You shouldn't take bait either. Also, don't kid yourself — He's not lying in a coma somewhere. There was no near-fatal accident about which he's going to regale you with once he's released from the hospital. *POOF!*

There are many reasons why a person chooses to 'ghost'. I can overanalyze it till the cows come home — Mebbe I laughed too much, my jokes weren't funny, he met someone else... Bottom line is, if s/he's interested, s/he ain't goin' anywhere. He just wasn't that into me (and took the cowardly way out).

I used to blame myself for various reasons: Am I not pretty enough? Not thin enough? Too tall? Too forward? After talking with many men who've had experience with online dating, though, I learned something that helped renew my self-esteem. It's simply this — everybody on those sites is talking to at least five other people in addition to you, and it's not personal when they disappear. You just never know if they were more advanced in conversation with someone else and so they dropped you to focus on that person, or if perhaps it was all an act until they decided they didn't really feel a spark. Mebbe s/he didn't have the cajones to tell you s/he really just wasn't interested, or that there's some other reason why they can't focus on you right now. Perhaps they met someone at a party, someone on another site, got busy with work and thought it would be rude to look you up later (sometimes they do!), hooked up with someone they thought they had something special with, suffered a loss in their lives and had to back off, just got tired of the whole online dating process, etc. The list of reasons to vanish is endless, but it may have absotively nothing to do with you!

I know I've dropped back more than once. I never liked telling my life story over and over again to strangers I knew I'd never see again. What's the point? It's never good to give out too much personal information right upfront anyway. I don't just mean your last name and address; that's a given. I mean hold onto your skeletons until you've gotten past a few dates and know this person is who s/he says s/he is, and will stick around! You don't want them knowing too many secrets of yours otherwise. Best foot forward!

Davey Downer

Case in point for putting your best foot forward. I met this man for dinner and it went well enough. I couldn't say we'd end up married one day, but we both agreed there was *something* here worth exploring. Our second date was far less fun for me. He seemed down, negative. At the end of the night, he confessed he had a serious personal problem on his mind and we talked about it as friends — in the car, into the wee hours of the night. I took a skeleton out of my own closet to show that we all have our crap, none of us gets out alive with an easy life.

Although I agreed to another date, over the course of the week I decided I just wasn't feeling it and so the best thing to do was cancel. I said that dating should be light and airy, fun and romantic! We were none of those things, but if he needed a friend to talk to, I could be that for him. He pointed out that good relationships start with friendship if they're going to last. This is true, however, we were going down a dark path and I was not romantically interested. We continued to meet for dinner as friends, except now I was his sounding board at my expense! What was I doing?! I began dreading our 'dates'. I would listen attentively, all the while thinking: That's very interesting — please, drone on! ZZzzzzzzzzzzzzz... If you're looking for compassion, you'll find it in the dictionary between chlamydia and constipation. UGH!

This continued for a couple of months, until things got progressively stranger. He was acting clingy and otherwise behaving oddly. One day he sent me a text saying he wanted to take my 15-year-old daughter for ice cream, "and you're not invited!" Um, OK… When I asked him what that was about, he immediately became defensive saying, "OH MY GOD! I can't *believe* you'd even THINK that!" I asked him what it is I was thinking. (Dafuq?!) A week later, he texted me at work to say he was at my house, wanted to give me a hug, "but you're not home." No, I wasn't — but my daughter was!! And he knew our schedules!!! I asked why *he* wasn't at work. He said he'd had a therapy appointment and my house was on the way home. It was not. NEXT!!!

Suffice it to say, I did not consider this a healthy friendship, seeing it as inviting drama and dysfunction into my life, which I do not need. Not fun or funny! There are boundaries, and he did not respect mine. It wasn't until he crossed a line with my kid, though, that I woke up and severed all ties. Some lines cannot be uncrossed.

The lesson learned here is that dating should be two people getting together for a fun time. The heavy stuff needs to stay locked away until you're comfortable enough with each other to share the secrets. This should be a no-brainer, but it turns out common sense isn't all that common. If someone is laying the dark stuff on you right away, it's a red flag waving!! Wish him/her well, and RUN.

The Weary Widower

I've dated a few widowers in my lifetime, and it was never easy for either of us. Obviously, the longer the person has been without his/her late spouse, the better your chances of enduring as a couple are. The newly free spouse is usually in a hurry to 'replace' the person s/he lost, doesn't want to be alone, and so he'll jump into something he's not truly ready for. Sometimes, they are looking for an instant family, or they are approached by someone else looking for that from the newly single person, hoping the vulnerability factor will be on their side. I found this weary widower to be sweet, kind, sexy and funny — at first, anyway. Little red flags started popping up all over the place, and, hard as it is (because we want what we want), I've learned not to ignore those.

Not only was he spoiling the hell out of his daughter — a typical move of fathers who feel sorry their child is now without a mother — but this meant little time for us, alone or otherwise. They are reluctant to leave their children alone, even when they are old enough to not need a babysitter. When I tried to talk to him about this, he made it all about money. He called me a gold-digger, suggesting I was like all the others — assuming he's rich simply because he lost a spouse. Huh??

OK, some people do have life insurance on their spouses — it's the responsible thing to do — but that does not mean you become rich when that person dies! If anything, I would expect that you are now in a lower income bracket because you don't have that second check coming in. If you did have life insurance, that only goes so far when trying to adjust to your new station in life, and you are prolly more broke than ever after medical and/or funerary expenses. Receiving Social Security benefits for your child also isn't going to make you rich.

The minute he said, "My therapist warned me about women like you!" I knew I had to run. Kudos to him for seeking help, however, I am emotionally available to begin a healthy relationship and shouldn't have to settle for anything less. Clearly, this man was not ready, and had some issues to work through. I had no problem saying to him, "I live a very comfortable life, so I don't need your money, thank you very much. While I would've welcomed your child into my life, I already have a child of my own — and she has a father. Also, I've owned my home since I was 23, so I think I'm doing OK. I'm pretty sure your therapist was referring to women who have nothing, and need a place to live." NEXT!

Seattle Surfer Bud

"Bud" wrote just to say he thought I was cute and sweet, too bad we lived so far apart. But when they put that out there, somewhere in the back of their minds they're hoping that you will respond and something will start up — a text buddy if nothing else. Well, like I said, I don't let the long-distance thing stop me if I feel a connection. We ended up forming a friendship, talked every few days for a couple of months, not really expecting we'd actually meet one day. He was a lonely widower, living in the boonies outside the city, and we'd spend hours on the phone sharing tales. Eventually, he suggested we meet. I agreed this warranted further exploration, and tried to figure out the best plan of action. Since he lived in a warmer climate, April vacation was the perfect time to fly, and then (if we hit it off) he would come to me in the summer. He said buy the ticket, and I did.

April was still about a month away, and we continued our weekly conversations. Two weeks before the trip, guess what? *POOF!* I'm always ready for anything, so I was not surprised when he pulled a Houdini. I knew the risk long before buying a plane ticket, and had nothing to lose really. It's not unusual for them to back out at the last minute, especially for a potential long-distance relationship (See Country Cole). Sometimes you just have to take chances in life! If nothing else, I'd be getting out of Dodge. My friend Erin was living out there at the time, so it was more a trip to see her anyway. I let Houdini #143 know that I

85

was coming to Seattle regardless, so if he (grew a sac) changed his mind, we could arrange a coffee meet and greet. Not that I'd want to meet someone who'd let me buy a plane ticket then disappear on me — I've got more self-respect than that! It was prolly more like morbid curiosity at that point. Erin showed me a great time while I was out there, so we unfortunately did not have a chance to stalk the coward.

Smarter than when I first started this madness, I was aware of all the red flags waving. Bud's picture was of a very tall and buff guy, very masculine. His young surfer dood voice did not match the photo, so I always had my suspicions. Could this be why he didn't want to meet — because he'd look nothing like his photos? How could he tell me he lied the entire time?! Must ghost now! Before buying the ticket I'd done a test run, sent a box of homemade cookies to his house. They weren't returned so I assumed everything was legit. However, when I put his address into Google Earth I got nothing but a big forest of trees. When I'd related this to him, he just laughed. Things that make ya go Hhhhhmmm…

Ironically, when I arrived at Seattle Airport to fly home, I was pulled out of line by Homeland Security. I thought mebbe it was because I was wearing my Patriots football sweatshirt in Seahawk territory, but no. They needed to dust my snow globe as it could be an explosive device! Same thing happened to me when leaving Orlando; I had a water-lined souvenir cup from Disney World in my carry-on bag. You would think the souvenir shops would clue tourists in to this little quandary when selling the things to travelers! Anyhoo, once convinced I was not carrying a bomb, they let me fly home — right into the Boston Marathon Bombing! Yeah. Monday, April 15, 2013. I caught the last train home before everything shut down.

Besides the obvious logistics of starting a long-distance thing, flying out is more of a risk than a regular meeting is. So much is invested, usually just by one of the two. I bought the plane ticket and got a rental car, and was lucky to be able to stay with Erin. I would not be staying with a strange man, nor would I have allowed him to sleep in my house if he'd come to me.

My friend Cindy's daughter started chatting with a man in California. I guess they truly connected, because she flew out there and didn't come back! She sent for her four kids and moved her entire life out there to be with him after only five weeks of being with him. While I don't condone this speed of light movement, I do maintain that when it's right, it's right, you know it, and we're not getting any younger. Why wait if you're so sure? They are very happy today, and I'm happy for her. Still, this could've backfired on her big time! She was one of the lucky ones.

If the situation were reversed — a man flying out to meet a woman, like the man from Alaska who offered to fly to my state — you'd have to set the ground rules upfront. I told Mr. Alaska he'd have to stay in a hotel. He spouted, "You expect me to fly out there, at my expense, and then stay in a hotel?!" Then he hung up on me. A gentleman would've understood, yet I can also see his point. Thing is, he's a stranger, like it or not, and has no business coming to my house. That is a rule which cannot be broken.

Want more irony? A while later, Erin told me about a Washington woman she knew who met a man online — a serial killer who'd murdered her!! The guy had flown in from Ohio "on business," took the woman to a baseball game, and then… When her ex brought their daughter home from weekend visitation on Monday morning, Mommy wasn't there. They found her in several places… He'd chopped her up and spread her around. Still think you don't need to follow the rules?

The Dog Walker

If they're still chatting via text or phone and not trying to plan a meet and greet after two weeks, that's a red flag waving. Some people just like having someone 'on the other side' checking in on them daily, or just feeling like they have someone. If you meet and it doesn't go well, you're back to being alone, and that seems to scare people. Maybe you even lied about your age and/or appearance, so meeting the person would expose you. Now you can't meet, and so you play the game until the other person calls you to the carpet. This man must have been one of *those*. He seemed so interested, long enough conversations on the phone and so on, for nearly two weeks. We agreed to meet for coffee one morning, and just needed to pick a place. He said he had to walk his dogs, would think about a good venue where we could meet, then call me later to tell me where to go. So I waited. And waited. *POOF!* Vanished into thin air!

There are no words of wisdom here beyond the "Sometimes people are just plain @$$holes!" rule. Would it have been so hard for him to say something like, "Sorry, I'm just not feeling it. Good luck to you." COWARD! I was not happy, and called him on it. Like who does that?! He said he'd given it some thought, and I was a night owl while he was a morning person, meaning this couldn't work. SO SAY THAT! Sleeping patterns can be altered, not that I'm so eager to change my life and self to be the perfect partner. It stands to reason that if you rock me to sleep early, I'm going to wake up early, and fall into that pattern with you naturally. But we never got the chance because he was a coward. Communication is key! Methinks he will be alone for a very long time if he doesn't learn to communicate effectively. Not my problem. He's off the planet.

The Nut

"It'll take me an hour and 40 minutes to shovel my walk, call you later."

Not a little over an hour, not two hours — an hour and forty minutes exactly!? This is what he said to me after we chatted for over two weeks and it was time to meet. Never mind I'd invited him to one of my comedy shows and he did come. The only problem is that he didn't tell me he was there! I got a text later that night telling me I had on a nice floral shirt — proof he'd seen me at the club. When I asked why he didn't make himself known, he said I'd looked right at him and must not have liked what I saw because I didn't say hi to him and just kept walking. Huh?

I assured him this was untrue — like how would I know it's you?! — and that I still wanted to meet him (despite the red flag waving). We picked a time to meet for coffee after work, and there was a raging snow storm that day. As a police dispatcher, The Nut knew the roads were too hazardous, already forty accidents across the state. He advised me to go home, as he was going to do.

After not hearing from him at what I estimated would be his return home, I grew worried about his safety and called him. That's when he said he'd call me in an hour and 40 minutes.... Guess where this is leading! He never did call. Must have had a heart attack while shoveling.

Saw him a year later at a fund raiser he was collecting tickets for. He said I looked familiar. Imagine that! I told him I do comedy, and waited — ah, the look on his face! <blink blink> Like how many female comedians do you know?! He'd assumed he'd seen me before, but no, it was my ad photos he was remembering. To diffuse the awkward moment, I asked him what I should do with the ticket I was holding. He said he needed my phone number for a raffle. With perfect comedic timing I responded, "Don't you have it already?"

I could've made him feel like a real schmuck, but why bother. Sometimes it's enough just to walk away gracefully — be the bigger person — leaving them in your dust.

Ben Button

This guy kills me. I had written to show interest, and he politely wrote back saying he'd met someone and wanted to give that a shot. This is a lie, often used by men who just aren't interested and don't want to hurt your feelings or just can't be honest with you because they (are liars) want to keep you on the back burner in case things don't work out with any other women. If he were truly serious about another woman, he would've hidden his profile in order to pursue her without distraction. If you don't hide your profile, you get people still writing — and mebbe you'd be interested in one of those women…

We live in neighboring towns. Still, imagine my surprise when he turned around in church (I'm not religious, was supporting my daughter in her faith) one Sunday to shake hands during the sign of peace, and there I was! Instant recognition on both our parts. His smile was bigger than mine, however. He lit up like a Christmas tree, clearly pleased with what he saw (I'm often told I'm prettier in person, can't take a decent photo to save my life). A week later, I got a "He's Interested!" message from the dating agency, which I ignored. Sorry buddy, you had your chance!

In his ad, his age was listed as 53, and he apparently had a birthday coming up. Except I noticed after that point he was now 52, when he should've just celebrated his 54th birthday. A year later, his ad still active, he was 49. I checked more recently; he's now 45. Most people age in the opposite direction; must be nice to be him. And yes, he still attends church.

People lie. Believe it. They lie about their age, their height, size, marital status, and Lawd knows what else! If they'll lie about one thing, you have to assume anything goes! You know it snowballs — once you tell one lie, you have to fib more to cover your lies. In that respect, it's not a little white lie — it's a major red flag! You ought not start a relationship off with lies.

Musical Mark

He'd listed himself as having an average body type. Pretty sure that 10-month gestational belly isn't average. Does he think I'm blind? He was fun and interesting, but in the back of my mind I kept thinking, What else is he hiding? What else did he lie about? Didn't I just go through this with the last guy?!

♥

NEXT!!

Screaming Scotty

We agreed to watch the Super Bowl together at an equidistant sports bar. While he was as handsome as his pictures, the façade quickly changed as soon as he opened his mouth. At first I wasn't sure if he stood a chance with me, but his fate was sealed when he started yelling at the TV — and I mean deep-throated senseless outbursts — to the annoyance of everyone around him. I wanted to crawl under the table every time he barked something stoopid! Not only did he keep calling out irritating commentary at every good or bad play, his voice was grating!! He wasn't even drunk! People kept looking at me as if to say, "Really? What are you doing with this loser?!" Next!!

Funny, I went to that same sports bar months later for trivia night, and across the bar I heard this rather abrupt and deep-throated senseless yelling... His date seemed amused (a match!).

Rhode Island is way too small. Just sayin'.

When people do things that irritate you upon first impression, pay attention. Ever notice, when you first meet someone, there's a little something that irks you, but you let it go because you like the person and it's seemingly no big deal? That noise she makes when she chews is kinda cute, really. But then the puppy luv fades, and suddenly you're surprised how irritated you are by her chewing with her mouth open! You think, How did I not notice that noise before?! UGH!! It was there all along, but suddenly it's a living, breathing thing that's taken on a life of its own! Point being, if it stands out to you at first, it's going to bother you later. Nobody is perfect; choose the irritating quirks you can live with! Scotty never stood a chance.

Biker Mike

Nice guy, I thought, just not for me. We'd had fun, so I agreed to keep seeing him, although I knew it would never lead to anything permanent. We went for dinners out, rides on his Harley and hung at his place. One night while watching TV, he "playfully" slapped my hand. I asked him what that was about, letting him know I don't enjoy pain. (There'll be no slapping of anything!) He slapped me again in response. I again asked him what that was for, this time more adamantly, and he went on about what a big baby I am. "That didn't even hurt," etc. Um, that's not the point! Yes, it did kinda sting because he was a huge man with big mitts, but what's wrong with this picture when you ask someone to not slap you and he slaps you *again?!* Helloooooo! I then asked, "What are you, FIVE?!" If it's like this after seven hours of dating —" He cut me off, "We've been dating for longer than that!" I corrected myself, "If it's like this after two weeks, what's it gonna be like after two years?" He said, "The same!" I got up and walked out the door. Buhbye!

This being a small state, I bumped into him about a month later. We were both on dates with other people, at an Asian restaurant where a band we both followed was playing. He must've spotted me, as he was (hiding) sitting at a very small table in the back room with his matronly ad date. I was actually there with an old friend — a very handsome, fine dancer at that. After watching my date twirl me around the dance floor for a short while, Mike slipped out with his date. Ah, the little things!

We again ran into each other the following summer while I was volunteering for a bike run — a fundraiser for the Station Night Club Memorial monument (Google it!). He paid the entrance fee, and I watched as my friend said, "Now go see Alison for your wristband!" If he wasn't sure it was me, now there was no doubt! He came over, extended his ginormous wrist in front of my face, and wordlessly stared off into space — just like a five-year-old. Glad I didn't hang around for that! Why stay longer than you should if it doesn't feel right? I'd rather be alone than deal with that noise!

Nothing wrong with being civil toward people you didn't hit it off with. Yes, it ended badly, but we (most of us, anyway) are all adults here!

Hey Sailor!

I'd agreed to meet at a popular restaurant chain's bar area. He seemed, over the phone, to be a successful and sweet man who had his act together. After the usual greetings and weather report, he went on and on about how people use him for his sailboat, "and that ain't happening anymore..." Little did he know, I would gladly accept a ride on his sailboat IF he offered, but I'm not typically a boat person and had no intention of using him for his sailboat, or his motorboat, or his catamaran (boasted all three).

When he noticed that the bartender and I were hitting it off (Barkeep was a budding comedian and had recognized me, asked questions), he suggested I get the guy's number. Then he suddenly had somewhere else to be — said he had to take some friends out on the sailboat — and left abruptly, saying he would be in touch.

Some ladies might believe that line, but I've gotten quite skilled at reading body language. Ladies — If he's staring at the floor instead of trying to kiss you, he ain't callin'.

Sometimes, that huge ego is just a front for an inferiority complex. Conversely, if his head is so big he can't fit through the door to leave, you've got a problem. Size matters. Show Mr. Narcissist through the double doors. Good riddance!

Lost Boy of Atlantis

I'm always amazed when men from far away contact me. "It's a little hard to meet for coffee!" is my typical response when these distant men ask my life story. And man, do I get tired of telling it! What are they going to do with this information anyway, since it's likely I'll never see them again — if at all?! Anyhoo, this one particular man — with amazing green eyes — happened to have his pilot's license, and flew in from Western New York with plans to take me to dinner on Martha's Vineyard! He even let me fly his friend's Cherokee Piper! How kewl is that?! Things were going so well! Unfortunately, there was a dark storm cloud above the island so he had to make the decision to turn back and dine on the mainland. These were the same treacherous conditions that took down John John's plane out there in 1999 — not worth taking a chance on!

Our dinner conversation revolved mostly around his past lives, and aliens — creatures he credits with giving us Greek architecture and the Lost City of Atlantis! He even backed this up with scientific evidence! Sometimes, you have to destroy what you've created so as not to leave a lasting slew of evidence when making a quick departure on the mothership.

He flew off into the sunset. Mebbe I'll see him in another life…

It's one thing to have a far-out conversation at first meeting. It's quite another when that's all you have to talk about and leave no room for doubt. While I'm always thrilled when it's not me carrying the entire conversation, I see a red flag waving when things like this happen. Try not to scare your date away. LB was surely interesting, I'll give him that, but as a potential mate he was a tad scary.

Tubby Teddy

This man listed his body type as "A few extra pounds". Now, I'm sure if he had written "Morbidly obese," women would avoid him like the plague. He was very charming and most likely knew he could win women over with his personality if they would only give him a chance and meet. While I did find him very interesting to talk to, and I battle with my own weight, I just wasn't attracted to him and couldn't get past it.

At the end of the meet, I started to clear my platter to bring to the return station (usually it's just coffee but we were foodies, so…) and he said, "Leave it, I'll get it!" I was surprised, thinking, Wow, what a gentleman!, but then I noticed he was wedged into the booth. I had arrived before him and chose a booth for us to sit in, and would've opted for a table had I but known.

I did feel badly for him, but not enough to see him again. I know, I know, I did to him what so many men did to me, but I work out hard and, while I will never appear "athletic and toned," I do not want to go backwards. I need a fit person who will keep me moving. Someone who plans on living a long, full, healthy life, and I don't think anyone should settle. You deserve what you have worked hard to get, you know what you want; might as well hold out for the brass ring.

Michael Sharp
if that's your real name!

This man did not disappear. Not really. He is, quite simply, the man of my dreams. His screen name was MichShrp11, so I call him Michael Sharp. I often wonder if he actually exists, or if he is what I'll refer to as a corporate plant.

Call me skeptical, but we know there are scammers out there who steal pictures from other sites and create a bogus ad with the intention of scamming lonely people out of their money after luring them with the promise of love. It's sad, it's wrong and it sucks. I know, as I've had it done to me (refer to Tony the Tiger). Still, it's a fact. So I wonder if companies benefiting from lonely people looking for love wouldn't find it beneficial to create a few bogus ads here and there of seemingly perfect people who would appeal to a large variety of subscribers. Think about it! I view Michael Sharp's ad on there and really, really like what I'm seeing. Not only is he handsome, he's into all sorts of activities as I am. He is well-spoken, describes himself as loyal and dependable, talks about loving just one woman — his soulmate. Appears to be a great dad, makes six figures, enjoys cooking and entertaining at home, loves his mama, dogs, blah blah blah. My soulmate! How many other women are pining over this flawless and potentially fictitious character? If it seems too good to be true…

In an attempt to find out if he exists or not, since his ad hadn't been accessed in over a month, I contacted the agency to inquire whether he was an active member. I was told, "We are not allowed to divulge that information. Here's where you can find a copy of our privacy policy." Huh? I did not ask them for his address or for (their #$%^ privacy policy) them to contact him for me, I merely wanted to know if he had an active account with them or not! If I'm paying them for the ability to access their subscribers' accounts, I think this is a valid request. I'm attempting to contact this person; is he or is he not going to get the message I paid to send?!

I'm sure some ads get far more responses than others, and when people tire of the process, they don't renew their subscription. What's to stop the agency from keeping the more successful ads running online for the exposure — even though they're inaccessible? The agencies are aware that people with hopes of contacting the (lapsed) subscribers will themselves keep their subscriptions active. Cha-ching!

If I could only choose one man to meet out of the thousands of ads I've read over the years, I would choose this one. Every ad I read now should make me feel the magic like Michael Sharp's did. This is so unfair, considering Michael prolly doesn't even exist, but it's also good in the sense that it makes you set a high standard for yourself. I've done what so many of us tend to do with these ads — focus on a great photo and/or the wording in the ad and get totally fixated on that person. We build him/her up to be something s/he's not — the seemingly perfect mate for us! Nobody else can compare to the god/goddess we've put on the pedestal. That's "The One"! I must have him/her!

Some of us are gifted writers who can be whatever we want on paper. Only when you actually meet the person can you tell if this is someone right for you, and even then you can be fooled (I'll refer you back to my three month rule). Before you agree to meet, however, you should talk on the phone. (What's a person hiding if s/he won't share a phone number?) You can usually deem someone worthy of a meeting or not when you converse live. If it's already not there after hearing a voice, why leave the house?!

If you meet and things are (even slightly) clicking, why not meet for a second time and see if things are more relaxed and the attraction is stronger?! Just because you didn't feel that instant ZING! doesn't mean it can't happen as you get to know the person better. We've all met people who became more attractive to us once we got to know him/her. I've talked to many women who said things like, "When I first met my husband I wasn't the least bit attracted to him! In fact, I felt nothing and didn't want to date him! But I gave him a chance, and thank God I did! I wouldn't trade him for the world now!"

I miss the days of old-fashioned dating, when what you saw was what you got, and you met in a social setting of like interests. This online process is backwards since you read then talk before you see and meet. But where's a person to go and meet others these days? Technology has replaced our social circles, and so we are now reduced to using technology in order to meet others. Except we are becoming less and less able to converse and socialize. I see this in the school-age kids and it gets worse each year. It's easy hiding behind a computer screen; not so easy when it comes time to get out there and actually meet. It can be a very frustrating experience, which is why we often need a break from the process, or give up altogether. Whoever invented online dating must be a masochist — or the grandest Houdini of them all!

Still, IT CAN WORK! If you see Michael Sharp, tell him I was askin' for him.

Not for Teacher

Not sure what was up with this guy, but when he found out I was a teacher, he rudely responded that he doesn't date teachers. Curious, I asked why that is, but he did not respond. Clearly, he had his mind made up about this. I've heard people say, "I'll never date a cop, too controlling, dangerous job, above the law, odd hours," etc. I've also heard people say they would never again date a musician or doctor, too egotistical and arrogant. But a teacher? I don't know. I'm a teacher, and because I have to correct bad behaviors, I can only assume this guy finds teachers to be too bossy or controlling. (Or, he doesn't like the fact that these women are smarter than he!) Personally, because I spend all day correcting behavior and barking orders, it's the last thing I want to do when I'm off the clock! It's certainly not something I would even want to have to do with a mate! AS IF!!

People have their hang-ups and you may never know what drives them, what toxic environment they were a product of, etc. It's not you! If s/he has some biased opinion of you beforehand because of your job (or whatever) and declines a meeting, be glad you dodged a judgment bullet.

Coupon Carl

Talking on the phone before choosing to meet definitely has its merits; can't stress this enough. I can usually tell right away if there's a spark here, or if a coffee meeting would be a colossal waste of time. This man was a bit too pretty and anal for my liking, just not my type at all, so when he asked to meet for coffee, I initially declined saying I didn't want to waste either of our time. He said that he never considers meeting someone new a waste of time at all, as everyone has his or her story to tell. People are interesting and worth meeting even if things don't ignite, could lead to a nice friendship, blah blah blah. So I agreed to meet him, and listened as he explained how much he can save by clipping coupons, shopping on a certain day, etc. "That's so interesting! (Zzzzzz) Go on!" I said as I stifled a yawn. (Eyes rolling) Forty minutes of my life I can't get back.

Trust your instincts! They seldom fail us if we listen! If it's not there over the phone, chances are HIGHLY LIKELY you will not hit it off in person. I had the strong inclination he and I wouldn't hit it off but I let a stranger talk me into meeting anyway. This man was clearly lonely for adult conversation, killing time away from his kids at home, and needed attention. Remember, your time is precious — no one can use you without your permission. Sometimes I feel like, "What if I don't go? This could be The One and I let him go!" Nah. Deep down, you know!

107

Cheapo Mon

Everything had a price tag for this guy. He couldn't mention a coffee or a car without telling me how much it cost, or how there was no way he was going to pay such-and-such for a cup of coffee, rotisserie chicken, etc. We never moved forward to a date, which is fine because I wouldn't be impressed with a breakdown of the dinner bill. He was obsessed with money, and nobody likes a cheapskate. Nothing wrong with being frugal and practical, but being cheap is just a flat-out turn-off!

This holds true for women, too. If a woman goes on and on about money, a man will run. Fast. He will likely think she is just out for his assets; nobody likes a gold digger (unless s/he's really hot. A fool and his money…). Some guys out there are still angry they lost a house to a breakup, etc. That angry, cynical thinking unfortunately gets thrust upon the next woman, who is innocent yet made victim to this jaded thinking.

Guys, beware. Yes, there are serial daters out there who will use you for a meal. Feel it out before you make a dinner offer. Yes, treat her like the queen she is, but also trust your instincts. You will know if a lady is truly interested or not. I get it, you have an inherent need to do the chasing, and we want what we can't have. If she uses you, it's with your permission. Start with coffee, choose to go from there if you click. Why not be creative in your first date?! It doesn't have to be expensive! A walk through the park, a picnic lunch, a bike ride. Use your imagination to win her over!

Non-fidelis

Wow. He got out of a topless Jeep wearing Teva sandals, nice jeans that showed off amazing buttocks, and a T-shirt that revealed an old USMC tattoo. I was hooked before he took off his glasses and I could see he was even more handsome than in his subtle photos. He looked the bad boy, but was not so bad from what I could tell. He sounded sweet and down-to-earth. This I knew before meeting him — from the caring texts he'd sent — and still I was pleasantly surprised. He stepped over my tongue and walked me into the café where he bought me a coffee and found us a booth.

Our conversation went really well. We seemed to have a lot in common, and talked for an hour. I listened intently, multi-tasking while lost in lustful fantasy as he rambled on about himself. Guys don't usually make it a point to ask the woman about herself. They learn about women when the female has an opportunity to (get a word in edgewise) interject about herself here and there. Men Are From Mars... Anyhoo, I felt this guy was a great catch and couldn't be happier that things seemed to click.

I knew it was a work day for him, so I was not at all surprised or put-off when he announced he had to leave. It was not abrupt or rude, and we couldn't stay there all day. We walked back to our cars as I pondered our potential. I'm a huggy person, so when he extended his hand, I asked for a hug instead. He obliged, and as we parted ways he said — as he turned his back to me and stared at the ground — "I'll be in touch."

Yeah, right! If body language were spoken, he was loud and clear! Then and there, I knew he wasn't feeling it and said as much. I suggested it was not fair to put it out there he'd be calling if he knew he wasn't going to. He just shrugged, smiled and said, "We'll see." You know when there's a mutual attraction; clearly he didn't feel as I did. Hey, it happens <sniff>. So, letting him off the hook, I said, "If it's not there, it's not there." And with a sheepish grin he admitted, "It's not there."

He suggested we could hang out as friends. Right. Sounds nice, and it does happen, but I saw this for the gentle letdown he meant for it to be. Didn't find what you were looking for — off you go!

I prefer brutal honesty. You're not letting me down gently if you've got me waiting by my phone (not that I would) for the disappointment to come. I'm a big girl, I can take it — give it to me straight! Have class enough to extend me that courtesy. I'm not going to fall to pieces if you tell me it was nice meeting me, there's just no real spark here. Chances are, I feel it too. Of course there might be hope on one person's end and not the other's — it happens — but be honest enough with yourself and the other person to own your feelings. There's nothing wrong with saying, "It was nice meeting you, take care!" I'll get the hint you're not going to call because *you didn't say you would*. THAT is letting me down gently!

Why give her/him false hope? What are they to do when you don't call? Some may go into stalker mode! Having a stalker is NOT fun! (See Tech Savvy Stalker) He did say there was nothing wrong with remaining friends — we could check out musical events together — and he encouraged me to join his hiking group. I called him twice to invite him to musical shows with me. The first time, he wrote right back to say he had to paint his ex-wife's house that weekend. The next time, it was more of a suggestion to meet me at a club, to which he never replied. I took that as my cue to forget it altogether.

I did join his hiking group, and let some time pass before attending a hike. During a hiking break I took a second to stretch my calves. He ran over to me with a hairy eyeball and fiercely demanded, "Are you cramping?!" I'd seen him talk to others similarly, and it occurred to me this dood had anger issues! Great catch indeed. Clearly, I'd built him up to be something he was not — a freakin' god. Bullet dodged there!

A wise friend once said to me, "If a man wants to be with you, he will be!" 'Nuff said. A guy who is interested will cross Hell and high water to be by your side, and no excuses will be made — he will FIND a way! If, however, he does not want to be with you, TAKE THE HINT! It's there, right in front of you. You want him to care, but he doesn't. Let him go, and DO NOT CHASE! You're better than that! Pick yourself up, dust yourself off, and MOVE ON!! You deserve someone who WANTS to be with you, who will treat you with the love and respect you deserve!

Tony the Tiger

You know, somewhere deep in your bones, no matter how good it sounds and feels, that if someone is calling you "baby" right away, moving very fast, asking you to take down your ad and wanting to email you via a secondary account through a lesser provider like Hotmail, something here isn't quite right. I learned a lot through this man about how scammers operate. He lived far away, claimed to be a widower with one child he's caring for, foreign born with no family around, earning six figures and often travels for work. He called every night around the same time, cutting us off around the ten-minute mark (There are others on his scammer schedule!), and kept trying to get me to Skype with him, saying his camera didn't work but he'd be able to see me. Hhhhhmmm… These are almost always the tell-tale signs your man (or woman!) is a scammer.

Tony said he was from Texas, originally born in Italy. I'm half Italian, have been to various Italian cities, have a good ear for sound as a musician and an even better ear for languages as an English teacher. I was pretty sure I'd never heard that dialect before — at least not in Italy! I teach in an inner-city high school where most of the students are African, so I was pretty sure he had the wrong continent. Also, every time I questioned anything that didn't quite seem to add up, he'd say something like, "Baby, I already told you! Blah blah blah, you weren't listening!" GRRRRR!!! How dare he blame me as a means of getting around

113

his lies! The only reason he managed to gain my trust was because I'd had a psychic tell me years before that the man I was going to marry had an accent and came from a southern state like Texas. I believed her because she was right about a few other things she couldn't possibly have known if she weren't gifted. Shame on me; believe what you will.

Anyhoo, I should never have given Tony my address, but I did despite my hesitation because he'd said he wanted to send me flowers. I don't even like cut flowers — I'd much rather have a man take me on a hike where wildflowers flourish around us, which is hard to do when the man lives three thousand miles away. Just sayin'. If a man wants to send me flowers to feel manly, so be it. I might get some info from the flower shop that he's actually from where he says he's from, which could be reassuring. He traveled for work, he'd said, so it wasn't impossible to meet for coffee eventually, and so I gave in.

When the flowers arrived, there was no return address, and of course I was skeptical. I called the florist and he agreed it didn't add up. He knew of a scam where people got ahold of a stolen credit card and bought the flowers online before the account was closed. No paper trail. More skeptical than ever, I asked Tony for his address. He'd said his birthday was approaching; I sent out a birthday card and it did not get returned to me, so I couldn't be sure that wasn't really his address. He didn't thank me for it, however, which was a good sign he never got it (because he didn't live there, even though it was a legitimate address).

As a literature teacher, I marveled at how perfect 'his' daily love poems were for someone who spoke English as a second language, and wondered where he was getting all these lovely gems. Just for $h!ts and giggles, I Googled one of them. What I found was astonishing! The first line of the poem I'd entered into the search bar brought me smack dab into a site exposing scammers! Evidently, these are Nigerian Love Scams. This explains "Tony's" African accent.

The trick is to gain your trust in just two, mebbe three weeks, and then pretend to fly out your way on a business trip. On arrival day, you get a phone call from the person saying something like, "Baby, I got pulled out of line at the airport by Homeland Security! They say there is a problem with my passport! I need to pay $1200 (or more!) in fees so I can be released. You know I'll pay you back, please can you wire it to me right away?" If you have half a brain, you will hang up and keep your money rather than sending it to a person you've never met, but it's scary how often these scammers are successful! They are predators preying on lonely people who would do anything for love.

A friend was going to wire her guy the money, and when she got to the bank, the teller asked her straight out, "How well do you know this person? Because there is a scam that people fall for…" She was livid, but of course there is no way to get ahold of the person and even harder to prosecute. Do yourself a favor and familiarize yourself with these online love schemes. Information is power! Most ad sites have a link for reporting suspected scammers. Use it! Spare someone else from having to go through this madness now that you know what to look for. We'll never stop them completely, but we can make their job more difficult.

FYI, I'd contacted someone from the scam site and inquired why Tony would want to Skype with me if I can't see him. She said if I'd taken him up on it, he would've tried talking me into taking my shirt off for him. You know, so he can get his rocks off while having to spend his nightly ten minutes with me while preparing to scam me. Let's get a little sexual predator crap in there before attempting to rob your money! Nothing wrong with his camera, he just couldn't risk being seen.

Tech Savvy Stalker

He was a very intimidating Middle Eastern man — the scary car bomber type. We agreed to meet for coffee at a café on the following Thursday, however, I'd made it clear I was not romantically interested, but would meet for networking purposes only, and we exchanged phone numbers. Suddenly, things changed. He was texting me all the time, trying to be romantic, no longer suggesting but demanding we meet for wine at my house on Tuesday instead! This was a deal breaker for me (red flag flailing!). I politely reminded him this was not what I was looking for, and that I was not interested in continuing our communications. He persisted in trying to persuade me to meet him, contacting me repeatedly via phone calls, texts and LinkedIn messages, all of which I ignored. (If they reek of desperation, RUN!) When it didn't stop, I blocked him in all ways. To this day, he occasionally checks out my LinkedIn profile, although he is blocked from contacting me.

A day or two later, my online dating account had been hacked. I found it no small coincidence that he was a computer programmer and now suddenly I was described in my profile as a 6'5" lesbian in Arizona. Not that there's anything wrong with that. But I was also described as earning over $150k a year, with a penchant for golf and cooking. Anyone who knows me can tell you this is the polar opposite of who I am! (Especially the cooking thing! It's not the how to, it's the want to — or lack thereof. Lots of guys cook these days so I don't see a problem.)

I guess he figured if he can't have me... It took a week for the agency to correct my settings, during which time I was receiving angry emails from women who were not gay, and complimentary letters from eager women who were seriously infatuated. I was breaking hearts all over Arizona!

Stalkers can be relentless and need to be shut down quickly. You need to firmly let them know, in no uncertain terms, that you have no desire to be in contact with them and they need to stop contacting you or there will be serious legal consequences! Rejection of any kind is not usually well-received, and people with stalker tendencies have an especially hard time letting it go. This is no time to be nice — shut them down firmly! Technically, to legally be considered a stalker, s/he must have hurt you or threatened to hurt you, but report it just the same if they don't go away — on the ad site as well as with your local police. Chances are, s/he has a prior history of stalking. In the digital age, it's easy to find someone if that person really wants to find you. How scary is that? Take it seriously!

Alison O'Donnell

Smooley

This man looked like modern day Eddy Van Halen. He had dyed black hair, which might've made him look younger if not for the poor job he did with the bottle, and the weathered appearance of his face, which indicated a lifetime of booze and cigarettes. Clearly this was not the man for me, but in my loneliness, I agreed to see him again after meeting. It's never a good idea to go to someone's house so early on, but we had already met in a public place where he'd bought an appetizer plate for us, so I reciprocated with a pizza at his place. I brought my dogs with me since we were planning on watching a movie or two and it would be a late night. His roommate (45 and pregnant from a man 20 years her junior) helped herself to the pizza without asking (I'd share, but ask! Right?) and sat down on the couch between us. If there were any remote ideology of romance here, it was now squelched. He later complained that my dogs were too energetic and I babied them too much (Ha! So not true! Red flag of his own insecurity).

A friend had actually dated him, and I learned several unflattering things about ol' Smooley. When he became too smothering, showing up at her house (stoned) at all hours unannounced, she felt the need to end things. His version of their relationship to me, however, was that she liked her dogs more than him (see a needy pattern here?), and lived too far (Haha! That didn't seem to stop him from coming by her house a few times a day, every day). I saw him months later, in a nightclub with a woman who looked

118

like him — cocaine thin and haggard from wear. A true match! Bullet dodged there.

Why settle?! It's tempting at lonely times, but you just know it's never going to last, and if it does you will be miserable anyway. Quality time alone would be so much more rewarding. Take up a hobby, keep a journal, ride your bike, join Meetups where you can find people who share similar interests... Anything to stave off the bug that makes us want to lower our standards! We deserve better!

Mr. Bojangles

This music man told me he'd bought an expensive dinner at a fine Boston restaurant for a woman he knew he'd never see again. In retrospect, he had known it would be a mistake as she had champagne taste and he was a minimalist. He felt rotten about it afterward, losing all that money for nothing, and decided that wouldn't happen again. From now on he'd meet the women for coffee. That's fine, just a coffee for me. However, I had a sense of deja vu. Here we go again, bearing the brunt of a guy who felt burned by the woman before me. Wasn't that all his choice?! (I didn't know any of this prior to meeting; seemed so sweet) She got a fancy meal, I couldn't even get a coffee!

When we met inside the café — a place he chose near him as there was a good distance involved — he'd said, "I'll hold the table while you go up!" You'd think he'd spring for a ^&#$% lousy coffee after I drove all that way, but no! When I returned with my coffee, he poured himself a free tap water. Yeah. We chatted in the cafe for a while (mostly about his misfortune in love, and his allergies. How depressing!). Cost him nothing; cost me two hours of my life I can't get back! Honestly, what impression did he think he'd make on me if that's how it is? Are you SO jaded?!

I'm not shopping for damaged goods here. I'm immediately turned off when a man says something like, "I'm never getting married again, screw that!... She took my house, she cheated on me, blah blah blah..." *She* is not *me*. I'm not the woman who wronged you! Don't I deserve a chance? Who's to say I'd ever do that to you, or that you'd suffer a second time?! Are you so pessimistic in the ways of love? If the other person is damaged goods, move on! It's not your job to cure him/her, and you likely couldn't even if you wanted to take that on.

Also, I will never again do the full drive and spend my afternoon being a sounding board. Meet halfway if he's not offering to come to you (I admit I'm always impressed when a gentleman insists on doing the drive). This isn't a jaded view so much as self-preservation. These people are strangers to you and you owe them nothing; meeting halfway is only fair. Allow ten minutes to see how the conversation goes, and get out of there if it's all about him!! I should've left him licking his wounds over his water (I'd say crying in his beer, but...). Live and learn.

Asian Snafu

I agreed to meet a Chinese man inside a trendy cafe. He hadn't said he was looking for romance, just someone to chat with about culture and other intellectual things. I was intrigued. He made himself known when I arrived, having already gotten his coffee, and had seated himself at one of the small tables. I went to buy my coffee at the service counter, walked to another counter for cream and sugar, and then sat down at the table.

That's when it happened. The scene unfolded before me like something out of a bad Woody Allen movie (debatable if there is a good one). Picture this in slow motion: I hear my name being called from afar. I turn to look across the non-crowded café following the trajectory of the voice and there he is — my eyes honing in and locking on my date. Steam coming from his ears. I look back at the man in front of me at my table, glaring, — and the realization sets in — I'm seated with a *different* Asian male. Yeah. Cue the crickets. Cut.

Both men stared at me wordlessly (there are no words…) as I shamefully made my way to the other table, like a scolded child. I mumbled a humble apology; nothing more could be done. Needless to say, our conversation didn't go well. In fact, the only thing to *go* was him.

Worst. Date. Ever. I have no advice here, other than mebbe arrive first, or sit first to get your bearings so you can (get your head out of your arse) memorize the picture of the person you're there to meet! Mebbe I needed a coffee before having our coffee...

Just be aware, some people make it a point to get to the designated meeting spot first in order to scope you out 'just in case'. It's not uncommon for someone to take a look and run before you have a chance to meet (See Beantown Bonehead). Shallow people abound.

Keep On Truckin'

This man had me. Super cute, intelligent, uber positive — what more could you want? He was a trucker, and the stereotype here is that truckers are drinkers. They won't drink the night before working or while on the job, as that could cause them to lose their CDL license, but that doesn't mean they aren't sucking them down on their off nights — closet alcoholics despite what they tell you. If you've never dated an alcoholic, let me just say they can be quite charming but are not known for dependability, are notorious liars and you are to blame for every little thing that's wrong in their lives (I refer you back to Yugo). Red flag waving, but we can't always say the stereotype is true. I like to give people the benefit of the doubt whenever possible (and usually get let down, not having trusted my instincts). Trucker seemed just as excited about meeting as I was, and said he'd call Thursday night to confirm our coffee meeting on Saturday. Guess what? Another Houdini! Since I won't ever chase a man, I let it go. Sure, I was disappointed, but the writing was on the wall. This type of person is clearly not dependable — not a man of his word — and therefore would make a lousy life partner. ¡Hasta lluego, bud!

Sometimes, Houdini reappears. Around two weeks after having snubbed me, a man may resurface with some lame excuse as to why he (blew me off) didn't call. Trucker said, "I was looking at your photos, wondering what happened. You're so pretty!" (Bait is cheap) I responded with, "What happened is, you said you'd call and didn't." Now he thought I'd taken the bait — he had me engaged in conversation, a start to luring me back. "Something came up," he said, "I was afraid you wouldn't see me."

Where to begin. OK, so let me get this straight — You figured I wouldn't be understanding so you blew me off, then decided two weeks later to see if there was any truth to that? You couldn't send a text at the time saying (you liked someone else more but it didn't work out) something has come up, can we please postpone? It's amazing how people will lie so effortlessly, and actually believe you'd actually believe them. Don't be stoopid, trust that this person is eating your dust because you are better than that! I didn't even bother responding. Trucker then tried to bait me with a response by asking, "How is your Walking Dead show going?" Really?!?

As my dad used to say, "You can't blame a guy for trying!" That doesn't mean you have to take the bait. Have some dignity. People like this are so not worth your efforts!

Little Boy Duh

If a man starts a conversation with one two-letter word, I figure that's not a very motivated person. I can do better.

It starts with "Hey!" or, more simply, "Hi."

Um, is that all ya got?

As mentioned earlier, when we get older and the looks start to fade, what else have ya got? You'd better be able to converse with your partner or you're in for a very lonely geriatric life!

This young man wrote to tell me he has a girlfriend, but he's coming to my town for a week and would like to hook up once, mebbe more if we click. While I appreciate an honest man, and I would much rather hear a straight-forward line than play games, I myself haven't wanted to hook up with a younger man, whether once or more. Call me just a girl, but I would much prefer the emotional connection of intimacy, instead of waking up feeling like garbage the next day — especially with someone young enough to be my son! Not. Interested.

Cougars, worry not. Once you take the "Hi" bait, they will be very blatant about what they are looking for. And, you can't blame a guy for trying! If that's your thing, go for it — so long as you check his ID to assure he's over 18!

Views will differ widely on this topic. Can't blame a guy of any age for trying. I believe it's different when the man is older. They see the age bracket you've listed as a mere guideline, and have nothing to lose by writing some clever lines to hook you in. Big picture: These men see themselves in their mirror as the high school football hero they once were. So while you're looking at them wondering what they think you could possibly see in them, they see themselves as the total package. They may have a better financial package than younger men, meaning you may be trading one package for another <ahem>. While it is possible to find a great guy who is still active in all ways and is financially secure, odds are his best years are behind him. They say age doesn't matter. No guarantee you yourself won't get hit by a Mack truck, or stroke out before him! Whomever you choose as a partner, then, depends on where your priorities lie.

If a woman is actively seeking a man much older than herself, it usually means one of two things. Either she is riddled with father issues and needs a daddy (red flag waving!) or she is looking for a sugar daddy. So long as the man is aware and doesn't have a problem with that, as it means he is scoring a beautiful young woman he can parade around, it's a win-win! If a woman seeks a much younger man, it is no doubt for one thing only.

Call it a bias. I think it's completely unfair that a man reaches his sexual prime around 18 while a woman is in her thirties. See any correlation here?! If a 35-year-old woman dated an 18-yr-old, people would rightamatically assume he's her son. But if an older man dates a young woman, people would think twice before assuming the relationship between the two. It's unfair, but the world is not ready for this double standard to end. I for one am OK with that. I just can't wrap my brain around dating a young man who looks — and no doubt acts — like he's my child.

Liar Liar, Pete's on fire

This guy seemed to have it all. If it seems too good to be true, it probably is? A quick Facebook search and I found this handsome man — in a photo sitting happily next to his beautiful wife, in their cute matching shirts — time stamped just two months earlier. Prior to this we had agreed to meet, so when he texted me a few days later just to say hello and confirm, I told him I don't date married men. He wasn't sure where I got that information, thought it was from a mutual acquaintance and assured me I can't believe everything I hear. When I told him I saw the pictures on Facebook, I was suddenly blocked from his wall, and I mentioned as much.

He claimed, "I did not block you, I hid my account. If you had asked me, I would have told you."

Huh? I'm supposed to think to ask him if he's married? I reminded him that his ad read 'divorced' and that he'd told me himself he'd been divorced for ten years! "That was from my *first* wife! If I had thought we were going anywhere in the relationship, I would have explained all this." All the while he was still trying to meet for a drink. Hhhhhmmm, really? Anyone else finding this all too convenient? I texted back, "You still misrepresented!"

His response? "As I said, IF I had thought we were headed anywhere, I would have divulged that information!" Oh, *well then!* How insensitive of me, eh? Like how do you justify such a thing?! NEXT!!

128

As people often do when caught in a lie, he snapped at me when I called him out — trying to make *me* look like the bad guy here! Hhhhhmmm, kinda sounds like an alcoholic mentality as well. (If you're unsure if he's a drinker, ask yourself — Did he offer to meet you for a coffee, or a *cocktail?*!) There was a time in my ignorant youth when I might've caved to his angry intimidation, but I've come a long way, baby! Married people are in NO position to date, PERIOD! They cannot offer you *anything* healthy. Why start an affair; it can never end well. Moreover, why would you want a cheater?! Do you really believe said player would never stray from *you*?! What's love got to do with it — cheating is a character flaw that you have zero control over. If he cheated on her, be assured he *will* cheat on *you*!

When I say cheater, I'm neither referring to the person who had a one-time indiscretion s/he deeply regrets (we're human) and learned from it, nor the person who stepped outside the marriage and immediately moved into the spare bedroom and got divorce papers rolling. I'm thinking of the players who run two (or more!) lovers at once without a conscience. No remorse, no morals. Who cares if he has (supposedly) been sleeping on the couch for a year now! He's married — end of conversation!!

Cute Construction Connie

This hunky handyman suggested we meet for breakfast on a morning we were both working. We had a nice meal and conversation, and seemed to hit it off well. When the bill came, he announced he'd forgotten his wallet, I'd have to pay, and of course he'd make it up to me. "Oh, look at the time! Gotta get back to work!" Instant buzz kill.

This is a common game. I've heard other women say it happened to them as well (But at the cost of a dinner! I got off easy with breakfast). I suppose some men get tired of being expected to pay for dates that go nowhere, which is why meeting for coffee is just fine. People sometimes get down on the opposite sex and decide to make them suffer a bit for their bad experiences. Hey, it wasn't *me* who burned you! ARRRRGGGHHH!!!

Sadly, this is just one of the many online dating games that make it so frustrating for those of us who are decent people truly hoping to meet someone special. While I do like to give people the benefit of the doubt, I was not believing him for a minute, and so there was no way we were going to go out again. I would've asked for separate checks but didn't want to see the waitress get stiffed instead of me. Of course the con artist said he'd call again, but guess what? Good thing I wasn't holding my breath.

If he were an honorable man who'd truly forgotten his wallet, he would've said so BEFORE ordering. Walk tall, carry cash.

A bit of trivia for you — the 'con' in con man does not stand for conniving, as most believe. It actually stand for confidence! Think about it — you would have to be fairly confident to pull off the scams con artists get away with!

Old friend

It's not uncommon to run into someone you knew in another life, like from your old neighborhood, high school, friend of a friend, etc. This person found me and was instantly sure we'd hit it off. We met for coffee, and he started telling me right away all the things we were going to do together, couldn't wait for our kids to meet, and so on. Ugh. Where to begin… Nothing is more put-offish than someone who reeks of desperation. Moving too fast is one of the cues that sends me running — FAST!

If there are kids involved, WAIT! Don't expose the kids to these folks until you are SURE things are headed toward something long lasting, be it friends or lovers. While kids are very adaptable and forgiving, it's unfair to let them get close to someone who's just here for a season. Or worse — someone who doesn't understand kids who would mistreat them with their ignorance!

A good rule of thumb, I think, if your kids are under 18 is to wait three months before introducing them to your new love. You know my theory — ***gotta pass the three-month mark to know if this thing might last.*** If you make it past that honeymoon phase and then want to get the kids involved, great. It makes no sense to introduce newbies to your kids right away, lest it burn out and you repeat the process, needlessly introducing the kids to all these partners who aren't, and never will be, an important part of your life.

I Think I Knew You Once...

Just like you may run into people who knew you years ago, you may also run into people you probably should've met just because you're in the same circle(s), but for whatever reason, it just didn't happen. I had a meet and greet with a sweet guy who had performed in bands as I had over the years. Turned out we knew all the same people — so how come we'd never met? Odd! Sometimes fate works in mysterious ways.

According to him, we had met in an online ad twenty years before! As he tells it, I had caught him in a lie about his job and decided not to pursue a relationship. He said he'd "always regretted it. I stopped lying after that." An honest person who still only works part-time, except at night now. Little opportunity for a social life.

I think it's healthy to have a friend of the opposite sex with whom you can bounce ideas and questions off of. My friend Bill, who could write his own book on dating — and prolly should! — is fun. We were both playing with online ads at the time, and would share laughs while comparing notes. It was at this time Bill passed on the wisdom of "The Three Tions". After the age of 30, he said, *anyone we date should have certain things in life: habitation, occupation and transportation.* (Bill later added a fourth caveat for my benefit — nobody wearing Hawaiian shirts after the age of 50 — especially on a date! BAHAHAHAHAHA, see Skip to the Loo!).

Most would agree that a middle-aged person should absotively have a place to live of his/her own (or at least a decent apartment in a decent neighborhood), a decent solid job (with a retirement plan), and a decent car (unless they're living in a big city where a car is a nuisance). If s/he doesn't have all three 'Tions', that's a red flag waving! Consider the guy who lives in his mommy's basement. He's not someone who's going to be a dependable, solid partner. Occasionally we all go through hardships in life that we need to bounce back from, but if he's still in the bouncing stage, he's in no position to offer you anything (but will surely use you for all you've got). You deserve a healthy relationship and don't have to settle for anything less!

I was taken in by this man's apparently honest, sweet nature and of course the attention I was getting at a lonely time. However, the writing was on the wall as far as partners go, so we could not be more than friends. While he partly had the Three Tions, he should've been more rooted at age 58 (he looked younger). Besides his unstable job and hours, he was living with an old friend in a spare bedroom (To his mother's credit, she'd kicked him out of the basement). As for a car, he was driving around in an unregistered vehicle. One night he got stopped by the police. Luckily for him, the officer let him go.

So did I. 'Nuff said?

farmer Jon's Close Encounters

Where to begin… People often don't look like their photos. Even if they put a date on them so you can assume they're current, it's not likely people are going to post horrific photos of themselves online when the point is to sell yourself in these ads. So you can imagine my surprise when my date showed up in his high-water farmer jeans <sigh>. That's not a look I'd admire if we were randomly passing on the sidewalk — and that's just the bad news from the neck down! My cousin was waiting in the parking lot with me for him, and we exchanged knowing glances when we saw him. I thought to run, but a deal's a deal; I'd agreed to meet and have dinner, so that's what I did.

Honestly, I sometimes feel like playing sounding board just isn't worth it. Really don't need the 'free' meal that badly. I *so* wanted to back out of our dinner at the Outback restaurant, and let me tell you, our conversation was *far out*. Farmer Jon had lots of UFO tales. To my knowledge, he was never abducted. But he did say that he saw other freakish things, and could tell me stories of people he knew who had been abducted, just didn't want to freak me out.

I sense there were lots of lonely nights in a southwestern desert before he'd moved to New England. While I like to think

135

we can't possibly be the only 'intelligent' life out here, the stories Farmer Jon told were a little *too* far out there! I like to think I'm open-minded, and who am I to say he and his friends didn't really experience these things. It just goes back to the whole 'behave on the first date' rule if you want to see this person ever again. Truth be told though, it didn't matter what we talked about; I'd never be sporting purple sneakers for or with him.

Porky Pig

This guy wasn't particularly handsome in his pics, but he did seem sweet and, well, ya gotta give the person a chance, yes? I've talked to many people who said they wouldn't have given their spouse a second look while passing on the sidewalk, but when they got to know the person, they fell in love with his/her personality, suddenly found him/her to be attractive, and was so glad they'd given the person a chance! So I give people a chance (if there are no red flags waving. Look for red flags).

Anyway, Piggy talked about sex all the time. Nothing wrong with a healthy sex drive, but have some class about it! When I half-jokingly suggested he was a pig, he erupted, saying all women say this to him and it's offensive! (Well?! Take the hint, pig!) He explained that he's a very sexual person and he'd make no apologies for it! OK, fine, I guess, if you can behave…

We met for lunch, then he took me for ice cream. The conversing went well. He played the perfect gentleman and was growing on me, especially when we then went to a book store and he managed to sneak a purchase of a small book set I'd been eyeing. (Bonus points!) Too bad he made a move on me as we later sat in his van (dumb move on my part!) and I was put off. Yes, he'd made it clear he's a very sexual person, but that doesn't mean you're welcome to me (in your vehicle, no less!) on the first meeting!!

Alison O'Donnell

Folks, if it looks like a duck, walks like a duck, acts and quacks like a duck and *tells* you it *is* a duck, well then... It's prolly a pig duck.

Pam's Roofier

My friend Pam met someone she really took to after having just two other ad dates. She was very selective, and would not meet anyone who was only offering coffee at the first meeting. She feels if a man offers dinner, it's a sign of good breeding, as he will always treat you right if he was raised that way. "Bob" bought her dinner.

I went to a BBQ at Pam's house and was looking forward to meeting her new beau. When he came in, she introduced us saying, "Alison, this is Bob!" I shook his hand and he said, "We met already!" The perplexed look on my face surely gave away my lack of memory, to which he further offered, "We had dinner in Pawtucket!" Oh. Crap. I had dated Pam's man before her! (RI is far too small…) I didn't even recognize him, as he wasn't wearing glasses when we met. No problem, we weren't breaking any laws. Two nice people who met on an ad date previously and felt no spark. Pam immediately laughed at the situation saying, "Thank you for not hitting it off!" We had a great laugh. Hey, these dates rarely work out romantically, but you just might meet a cool friend to hang out with!

That could've been an awkward situation, but as I often say, we're all adults here. She later told me Bob was embarrassed, but I don't see why. We didn't even share a peck on the cheek after meeting!* No harm done at all. But it wasn't always that way for Pam!

On her first ad date, she met a man in Newport for dinner. She says he was nice enough, but she just wasn't feeling it. She went through with the date, following him to a bar after dinner for a cocktail (where his nephew was the bartender), and suddenly she wasn't feeling well. She excused herself to the ladies' room, where she realized this was not normal; she'd never felt this way before. Spinning head, sour stomach — she truly felt her date had slipped something into her drink when she wasn't looking! When she told him she didn't feel well, he suggested she follow him to his place down the road where she "could lie down". Umm hmmm! I shudder to think what could've happened if she'd had more of that drink.

I've never experienced anything like that, but felt it was important enough to put in here. As a rule, I don't drink when I'm with a stranger. I'm not a big fan of alcohol to begin with, and since I'd likely go home with whomever is on my left after three drinks, I know not to imbibe when on a date with someone I don't know. I think it's a good rule of thumb to stay sober for just such occasions as this. I suppose it's possible for someone to slip a 'roofie' (general term for date rape drug, the sedative Rohypnol originally) into your coffee, but far less likely. Keep your guard up, and never leave your drink unattended!

*When leaving these dates, it can be confusing if there's to be a handshake or hug, a kiss, etc. My friends have told me they have rules… One won't hug, most of them won't allow a kiss. A handshake might even be going too far for some women, whereas the men… If they like you, they WANT to kiss you. Is that a bad thing? I guess not — so long as *you* want to kiss *him*! It's good to establish a rule and stick to it. Depends on how well the date went then, eh? Use discretion. I'm generally a very hands-on person — hugs are encouraged whether it was a match or not. However, if it was a bad date or I got a bad vibe off the guy, I ain't touchin' him! Only you know your own comfort zone. Control is yours.

Game Boy

The game doesn't change, only the skill level of the player. They think if they can get you into an apartment — theirs or yours — they're one step closer to the bed. I told this gamer I was a federal agent, not a lie since I was working for the Postal Service, but he naturally assumed FBI or something. When he asked for proof, I pointed to my government car's license plate. He asked what my mission was, since I was living in a hotel (I was on special assignment for over a year, domiciled away from home). Of course I had to reply with, "Well I could tell you, but then I'd have to kill you." He laughed, but it made him a bit more hesitant to want to be alone with me in a room — one with a bed or otherwise. Mission accomplished.

While you can't blame a guy for trying, there's more than one way to say No. Might as well have a little fun with it!

Alison O'Donnell

Blind in Boston

I've always had a soft spot for the underdog. Who is to say that someone with a missing body part isn't the one for you? There was a time when I would give anyone a chance at least. This man was very nice, a professional, classy guy who just happened to be going blind. He was legally blind at this point, couldn't drive but that wasn't a big deal in the big city. He was familiar with the bus routes and met me at a fancy restaurant of his choosing. I was impressed he'd spend so much on a stranger, and could only imagine he was as generous as he was successful. Or — as my friend Jeff would say —"All guys wanna get laid! That's ALWAYS their goal! The ugly ones just have to try harder." This statement never left me, and, funny as it sounds, does ring true to a point. I wisely considered that mebbe this man was doing what he had to do in order to get me into his bed at the end of the evening.

After the meal he'd asked if I would drive him back to his place so he wouldn't have to take the bus. I sensed no danger, and it was the least I could do considering the tremendous meal he'd treated me to. Sure enough, he encouraged me to come upstairs and check out his of-fice. I *just had to* see what he'd done with the place, he said. Flashback to another man I'd dated in Boston around that time, who *just had to* show me his windows... I politely declined, thanked him for a lovely evening, and said goodbye with a handshake. That pretty much sends the mes-sage that he's not only sleeping alone tonight, he's not expected to call me again.

♥

Can't blame a guy... Just be aware of the very many cheesy tacks men will lay for trying to lay with you! The choice is yours; *be aware of your surroundings* and play it safe! There are rules!!

Tippernaught

This guy seemed so sweet, and he was everything I like physically, so I didn't mind that he was an hour drive away. I also let it slide that he had two gorgeous female roommates, although I did wonder why neither one of them grabbed him up. Ah well, not every person is meant for you. My ex-husband was hot and seemingly sweet, but it got me nowhere. While I do believe you should be attracted to your mate, looks aren't everything. But I digress.

As always, I went into this date hoping "this is it!" yet having no expectations and keeping eyes wide open for my own protection. He might've *looked* attractive, but right away he started complaining about the fancy restaurant (which *he* chose), how expensive it was going to be (turn-off!), the distance between us, his bitchy roommates… Ugh! I often find myself being a sounding board for lonely, pessimistic guys who drain my energy with their negative whining (and they wonder why they're alone!), me-meisters who unload when they get a sympathetic ear. I'm often too polite to vacate, but in my head I'm thinking: I'm neither your shrink nor your mama. If you're looking for sympathy, you'll find it in the dictionary between *$h!t* and *syphilis!*

We got through dinner, and then the bill came. I offered to pay half; to my surprise, he declined — then proceeded to snivel about the amount, and how these dates are killing his budget, carp groan gripe… What really turned me off, though, was when he dropped three dollars down for the tip, saying that tips are arbitrary and that's all she was getting. As he slumped ahead of me toward the door, I slyly dropped a ten-dollar bill on the table. Our server gave me a knowing wink.

    I went into that date looking forward to meeting someone special, and what I found was anything but. It's amazing to me how this can keep happening! I believe I've screened my date so well, no red flags, yet who I meet in person is so not who I spoke to over the phone. It happens. I suppose it boils down to a combination of them being on their best behavior at first, and me being the trusting fool who puts them on a pedestal before meeting. NEVER lower yourself, cow down or think you're not good enough!

Dr. Jekyll, Hyde!!

Attractive, smart, sweet gentleman, successful, and totally into me — like a science project. He was an insurance adjuster but had always wanted to be a mental health therapist, asked a lot of personal questions about my dark childhood. Generally speaking, I've learned that many counselors took on their role because of their own skeletons. Since they themselves are dealing with deep-rooted personal issues, they want to make others well. Kinda like the way some comedians are usually alcoholic, divorced, depressed druggies (not me, just sayin') who work to make others laugh so we can feel better. It's a survival mechanism — we survive by living vicariously through others.

Turns out my man had a mom who wouldn't leave him alone, constantly demanding his attention and favors, which was preventing him from having a woman in his life, or having a life at all. Mama pulled the marionette strings from Florida on a daily basis. Stressed beyond the norm, he'd developed the nervous tic of scratching a specific spot on his forehead, practically boring a hole. By now he must've reached China, if his mom is still alive, as I doubt anything but her death would release him from her clutch.

Your parents' job is to raise you to be an independent adult, to go off and start your own family. That hole he was boring into his forehead was a major red flag waving. Yes, he was everything I look for in a man, but I didn't think there was room in his bed for the three of us. It's one thing if your mom is disabled and really needs your help. It's quite another when she lives 3,000 miles away and manipulates every aspect of your life from afar.

He also had a bad back — a slipped disc after moving office furniture — and was on leave from work. This limited his pay so he wasn't able to ask me out again any time soon, he'd said, but really wanted to. He walked me to my car, holding his umbrella over my head, gave me a nice hug and asked me to stay in touch, please. About a week later, he called and we chatted briefly. I'd mentioned I was looking to replace my TV, and he said, "Let me know how the new TV is!" Bait. I bailed, as I knew I could never have what I wanted in him. As great as he was otherwise, we could never have a truly healthy relationship due to his mommy issue. Mr. Hyde failed to hide from his puppeteer. He didn't have the fortitude to cut those strings — the ties that bind — which effectively made him unavailable.

Being a Mama's Boy isn't always a bad thing. It means they love and respect their mothers, and that carries over to most other women. If he's taking care of his mom in her old age, chances are he'll always be there for you when it counts too. Just make sure she's not a battleax who consumes all his mental and physical energy! A man in this position will likely engage in projection of guilt onto other women because of his controlling mother, for whom he never measured up despite being the perfect son in every conceivable way. Damaged goods; move along!

Chowdahead

With no identifiable red flags upon our phone conversations, we agreed to go to a Renaissance faire together. That was a huge gamble, as you don't want to be stuck spending an entire day with someone you're not clicking with, but all relationships involve some risk, a leap of faith (Still — go for the coffee!).

There was a good distance between us, which he didn't seem to mind, and I gave him directions to come get me so we could do the drive to the faire together. He arrived late, and was apoplectic when he pulled up (a cop parking under the No Parking sign, on my *lawn* no less!). When I questioned his arrival time, he immediately went into angry intimidation mode, blaming his tardiness on my bad directions. I was quick to point out to him that, had he followed said directions, he would've come in from the opposite direction! (Angry intimidation is a thing — beware! Red flag furiously flapping!!).

I would've (and prolly should've) bailed right there and then, and I think he sensed this (could have had something to do with my daggers of death glare) so he wisely changed his tone and opened the car door for me. We drove on in relative quietude, yet both aware it would behoove us to be civil as we still had hours to go.

When we arrived, he bought himself a chowder bread bowl, the creamy white juices solidifying on his face. I didn't tell him because I (disliked him) already wasn't attracted to him and wanted it to stay that way (Don't judge — you weren't there!).

On to the jousting. My drippy date fell asleep during the cacophonous festivities. Yeah. I didn't wake him as it wasn't my fault he was missing this expensive spectacle. When the show ended, I was amazed he didn't wake as the hoard strode past us. I continued to let him snore as I soaked up the warm autumn sun and otherwise peaceful solitude. The ride home was equally quiet, as I didn't want to give any false impression I was the least bit interested in a second date. We said our goodbyes and I let him down gently.

At least I thought I had. A month later, I received in the mail a large printout from him — the official rules for playing Dungeons & Dragons. (Dafuq??) I did not attempt to contact him to ask what this was about. *Three months later*, he called to inquire if I'd memorized the game rules so we could play. (HUH?!) I told him I was surprised to hear from him since we were not dating, and that I had no intentions of dating him either. To this he responded, "Well thanks for clarifying. It makes things easier." Okay then!

I've learned not to question madness. You can neither make sense of the nonsensical, nor rationalize the irrational. Some of these folks are delusional and any inch you give them will equate to a yard — an open door in their minds. Close the door and don't look back!

Casket Casey

This poor man was dying. Yeah. Said he had a degenerative disease and just wanted to experience love one more time before it was too late. I was nearly tempted to help him out with that, however, I knew this would be an unhealthy relationship for *me*. Nice for him, but what a lousy position to put myself in!

While my heart went out to him, he was a stranger to me. Taking on something that large was not my problem. Accepting that date would have been a codependent move, and I'd taken great steps to remove myself of that habit (Codependent No More, by Melody Beattie, changed my life forever!). In taking care of self, I know I deserve more and cannot take on that mental gravity. It doesn't mean I can't be sympathetic. I would've met him for coffee and been a friend. Mebbe. If he hadn't gone *POOF!* No, he didn't disappear because he died. I knew he had roughly one year to live (assuming this guy wasn't pulling some scam — and we know those types exist!), and saw revisions to his ad which told me he was still actively seeking. If he was legit, I wonder if he found what he was looking for.

Repeat after me—IT'S NOT YOUR PROBLEM! Be compassionate in life, absotively, but *take care of self. You deserve to be happy, you deserve a healthy relationship. Don't settle.*

Ever heard of the Reason/Season/Lifetime moral? It goes something like this — ***People come into your life for a reason, a season, or a lifetime.*** If you meet someone for coffee, don't click romantically but learn something you needed to know at that time in your life, there was a *reason* you met that person when you did (When the student is ready, the teacher appears). If you date someone for about three months, have some fun and learn more lessons — that person came into your life for a *season*. And then there are the people — family and friends — who are by your side for most of your *lifetime*. These people are also there for a lesson, connected by some invisible vine you are unaware of.

Don't take any of these relationships for granted, no matter how long or short they last. Embrace the lessons and the love!

GUY from NY

Another man from far away. You talk on the phone, sense a possible connection, and tell yourself the distance can be overcome for the right person. Guy took a train into Providence and we made a day of it. Because it was winter, and we'd exhausted all outdoor activities by the end of the day, I did bring him home to warm up. I hadn't noticed until he was in my familiar surroundings what an odd duck he was. He made comments on some of my furnishings, asked if he could take a box fan home because he'd need one this summer, said he'd build me a better computer. Perhaps the oddest thing of all, though, was when he used the bathroom — and didn't come out for over 20 minutes! I could hear little moans coming from inside and asked him if he was alright. He said yes, was just reading a magazine…

When I dropped him off at the train station, he left it that we'd stay in touch and see where this goes. But the magic was gone, he was just too odd for me. I couldn't go any further, and told him as much. He didn't seem to get it though.

One day, about three months after we last spoke, I received a computer band thingy in the mail. I had no idea what it was for. He followed up with a text, and when I asked him about it, he said to put it aside for the computer he's building me. Yeah… OK, in all fairness he *did* say at one point he would build me a computer, but I figured that deal was off the table when we stopped dating. Also, if I'm going to get sporadic pieces in the mail bit by bit, the thing would be antiquated loooong before it ever got built, eh!

A month later, I received a computer mouse. I emailed him to ask what that was for. He said to hang onto it, he's building me a computer... I reminded him we weren't seeing each other anymore. A month after that, he sent me some floppy disks. I again contacted him to remind him we haven't even been in contact, it's over. He again insisted he's building me a computer... I made no further attempt to contact him, having had some experience with this already (See Chowdahead) and knew just what to do — absotively nothing!

Long distance relationships are difficult enough for anyone to maintain, so starting one based off the Internet is even more onerous! Looking back now, I realize what a foolish decision it was to trust a traveling stranger in my home. His was not my burden to take on. Luckily, he was not an axe murderer or rapist, however, he was socially awkward. It could have been a very tragic incident. He definitely had stalker traits.

Bait is cheap. Psychos abound. Don't take the bait, lest you have to deal with a stalker — or worse!

Mr. Esquireless

Sometimes folks mean well — really want to meet someone special and start a relationship, but they're just too busy with work (or life in general) to get things rolling. This man was a lawyer who had a full caseload at the moment, and kept bumping our meeting up to the following week. Then there'd be depositions out of town, night meetings, conventions, etc. etc. etc. Each time he had to cancel he'd say something like, "I haven't forgotten you!" and "I really want to meet you! It'll happen!"

On the few occasions we actually spent a little time on the phone getting to know one another, it was all him. Telling me how wonderfully talented he is at his job. Mebbe he needed to pull the *Esq-wire* out of his arse!

Charming. I'm sure he was a nice man, however, if you have no time for me, what are we doing here? I'm not looking to be your something to do on the one night a season you're available! He'd pop in about once a month to remind me he exists, then mebbe once every two months, until it ran its course altogether.

People mean well. They really want someone in their lives, they're just too busy. It feels great having someone check in with you every day, even better feeling like you have someone waiting in the wings for when you are free. But it's not fair. If you're not available for a relationship, be honest and check the box that says "just friends" or "dating only". You're not available.

Skip to the Loo...

Shifty Skippy was an odd duck, to say the least. It was evident in the way he spoke, the way he lived his life, the fact that he'd fast for two days and eat on the third. Also, it's always a major red flag to me when your kid(s) avoid you. He was perturbed that he had to support his daughter until she turned 26, and even angrier over the amount of alimony he paid his ex-wife each month. He joked it would be cheaper to hire a hitman so he'd be free of the payments for life (or until she remarried, which she likely wouldn't do just to spite him).

Speaking of jaded! If someone is constantly talking about his ex, it's time to go home! Clearly he's still obsessed with said ex, has pain s/he needs to deal with, and is in no shape to offer you anything! Move along!!

Anyhoo... He had money but dressed funny by choice, bragging about how he shopped at second-hand stores (Think bargain basement Hawaiian shirts. It's why my friend *Bill felt the need to add "and no one over 50 wearing Hawaiian shirts!" to the Three Tions!*). This was during the hottest part of the summer, and he'd extended an invitation to his home to use the salt-water pool and house while he wasn't home. Weird. This was a major clue that he has a warped sense of boundaries. I was a perfect stranger!

This being a small state, right after our second date, my friend Jen told me she was chatting with this quirky guy called

Skip… We compared notes and, as she wasn't going to pass an opportunity when I had no claim on the man, she was ahead of my curve as I'd shared some good info about him that she could use to her advantage. As a result, he thought she was a better deal and Shifty Skippy went *POOF!* Bullet dodged!

Our tale doesn't end there, though! There's a neat Movie Night in Providence where they project great old movies onto the side of a building for free every Thursday. It draws an eclectic crowd. Bill, who is very affectionate, offered to hold a spot for me if he got there first. I spotted Bill right away, and guess what? The place he'd saved for me was right. Smack. Dab. In. Front. Of. Skip! (Have I mentioned my very small state?) Like what are the chances?! I couldn't have planned that one any better if I *tried!* Bill gave me a big kiss hello, and I fully admit I was enjoying this gift immensely.

Because we are close friends, it was natural for Bill to talk close, keep his hand on my knee, hold my hand, etc. And we had lots of laughs, which is something Skip and his plain date (who was *not* Jen) didn't do once. I overheard them having an intellectual conversation about something odd, like the electric system in Germany <yawn>. They, too, were sharing a blanket, but unlike Bill and me, their chairs were a foot apart and their clasped hands were kept to themselves. Bill was given a soothing head massage, and I was in seventh heaven knowing that Skip (who incidentally pretended he didn't recognize me and didn't say hello) was seeing all this.

At one point, Bill said he was tired and wanted to leave during the second movie, but didn't want Skip to think I'd been ditched. I said *No no, this is good!* He will think we're leaving to go get lucky — something Skip surely wasn't going to get that night! It was perfect! Ever the gentleman, Bill helped me pack up my chair and other items. Skip became visibly irritated by the obstruction, dramatically bobbing his head back and forth even though Bill wasn't even blocking the view at all. I looked right at

Skippy and laughed; he was *still* avoiding me! There's a certain satisfaction in knowing *he knows!* The wrestling bell goes off in my head signaling the final round defeat. Bill, oblivious to all this, sweetly took me by the hand and we walked off wearing big smiles. It's the little things, teehee!

As for Skip and Jen, they were hitting it off via email (and he'd invited her to use his pool while he was at work…). Yet there he was with this other woman (who might as well have been his sister, but wasn't). Ignorance is bliss, and he was free to date, but I felt Jen should know so I told her. They continued to email until it petered out, having never actually met. Sometimes, the thrill that goes along with fantasizing is all you get out of it.

The nice thing about fantasizing is that it never lets you down. The fantasy is always better because it's always perfect! It works out in your favor *every time.* And while I suppose I could abide a Salvation Armani wardrobe on my man, I cannot tolerate someone who knows no boundaries.

Joker, Smoker, Midnight Poker

(Poker? I hardly know her!) Our first meeting went OK. We agreed to meet for coffee at Panera. Assuming he was there already, I texted him to *Watch for my dramatic entrance!* He texted back, *Watch for mine!* I turned around and there he was, right behind me, having just entered after me. Good for a laugh, which is always big with me. Excellent start! He paid for my coffee and we found a booth.

Once settled, we somehow got into a deep conversation about things like ghosts, psychics, etc. He seemed enthralled. When he said he'd call again but didn't, I later asked him why via Facebook, since he was staying in touch otherwise. He felt I'd shared too much info on the first meeting; always wise to put your best foot forward in the very beginning. WTH?! I thought he'd enjoyed the conversation as much as I had, but instead I'd let a seemingly great guy slip through my fingers over something totally stoopid.

We remained friends, and he even surprised me one night when I was out with my gal pals at karaoke (he'd seen my FB post about it). We later shared a nice hug goodbye, but it was still clear we wouldn't be dating.

Not long after, I had an extra ticket for a comedy show, and invited him. He said, "Only if I can buy dinner first." Sold! He picked me up at my place (not a problem at this point), we had a nice dinner and drinks at a trendy place, and then off to the comedy show (more drinks for him). Afterward, he bought a round of drinks at a neighboring venue for my comedian buds!

Despite the later hour, it was the weekend, we were both night owls and we didn't feel the fun was over just yet. We drove to a local casino and sat at a Black Jack table. At one point, I went to the ladies' room — and discovered I'd hemorrhaged. Yeah. One of those lovely menopausal moments that catch ya by surprise at the worst possible time! I cleaned up as best I could, and returned to the table. Here I found him snapping mercilessly at a little old Asian man (who never so much as looked up) because he didn't like the play the man had made. (Was this the booze talking, or…?) I guess the man hadn't followed the general table rules of Black Jack. (Why do you owe anybody anything when you are gambling by yourself? Rules are rules) Up till this point, the night had been fun. He'd been so sweet and generous earlier, but that doesn't erase the crazy. Time to go…

When we got back to his car, he opened the door for me and I immediately noticed I'd soiled his seat. Yup. Brand new sports car… Leather seats, praise Allah, easily cleaned with a wet napkin before he even got around to his side. I felt obligated to tell him, however, in case it happened again. He said it wasn't a problem and proceeded to drive me home. At 90 mph. I got a quick hug goodbye, and he couldn't get out of there fast enough, peeling out of my driveway (2am, in my quiet neighborhood). I don't think he had a problem with menstruation as a rule; I think he was ticked he wasn't going to get lucky! He'd rented a hotel room for the night (Can't blame a guy…) since he (wanted to score) knew he'd be drinking, didn't want to do the drive home (about 40 minutes), and had friends in the area he wanted to spend the next day with (Gotta be out by 5am?).

We actually remained friends, mostly just on FB, sharing jokes and whatnot. Since it's a small state, though, we bumped into each other at a musical venue while with others, and it's likely to happen again. I'm sure I could call him right now and tell him to "Buy my book, you narcissistic bastid — you're in it!!"

The nicest thing about this man is that he was sincere enough to give it to me straight. He'd told me about a great woman he'd dated but dropped because he wasn't sexually attracted to her. Just couldn't get past it. This was his way of telling me that's why we weren't dating, and he suggested this: "You can't understand why some men don't want you since you're so nice, smart, pretty, whatever. *Find someone who wants what you have.*" In other words, only a man who likes a woman with an ample body would be attracted to me, and I'm told they're out there. Don't hate the player, hate the game! A man must be attracted to you or it ain't happenin'.

Give That Guy a Hand!

My friend Barry chatted with a sweet woman named Lisa, and they decided to meet for dinner. He headed over to her place (turns out they had mutual friends — small state — so she trusted him) and, while cruising along the freeway — he ran over a human hand! Yeah.

I can't make this stuff up, folks! Turns out a man had 'escaped' from the local loony bin and the unfortunate soul lost his life while trying to cross the freeway. Barry arrived at Lisa's door sick to his stomach. When she opened the door, she remarked, "You look like you've just seen a ghost!" In essence, he had. When he finished regaling her with what had happened, he admitted he had no stomach for eating and simply couldn't go through with dinner. Of course she understood, and they had a nice lengthy chat instead to distract him from the pictures in his mind.

Today they are married. Some couples defeat the odds!

The Doctor is In—sane!

This man was going through a prolonged, very bad divorce and needed a sounding board. Yeah. When I was able to get a word in edgewise, I told him he was in no position to date anyone right now. He agreed and offered me the opportunity to go out to dinner with him occasionally as friends. No thanks. I'd rather pay for a quiet dinner alone. The older I get, the more I'm all about the quiet.

Temporary insanity sets in when you're going through a divorce. Most experienced people will admit to this. Feelings are crushed, tempers run high, people need sounding boards in order to vent. I'm not your venting vehicle. I'm here for a fun date, trying to meet someone special I can converse with freely. If I'm just listening to you drone on about your troubles — what a biotch your soon-to-be ex-wife is, where's the fun in that?! Take care of your business, and when you're emotionally available for something more, THEN you are free to date!

Cartoony

Thought he was all that. I chose not to meet him because I picked up on the arrogance factor. I recognized him from his photos, standing at a kiosk in a local mall soon after, and did a double take. What a joke! Shorter, wider and really not all that. He'd completely made himself sound like the perfect man in his ad, so I was very surprised to see just how far off he really was in person. Too bad profile pictures don't come with the disclaimer you see on car mirrors: Caution! Objects may be squatter than they appear!

I've talked a little about how some will fudge their bio in order to sound more perfect, and I've talked a bit about some being shallow, so here I'm going to point out that it's what's *inside* that counts! Clearly this man thought very highly of himself, but he was still online two years later (same old photos!), likely because he never quite found the perfect woman — and I do mean PERFECT. He's a perfectionist and not willing to settle for less. Reality check — he's going to be alone a long, long time.

OK, hear me out. I know I say you don't have to settle, and I know that you have to be attracted to someone to a point if things are to move forward, but I allow that a person can win you over with personality if given the chance. What cannot be achieved is human perfection! Remember, there's a difference between "she's perfect!" and "she's perfect *for me*!" If he's an arrogant liar, he's not perfect for anyone healthy.

Guys who hold out for the Barbie dolls seem to fall into one of two categories. If they are addicted to the initial infatuation stage, they will feel the high for that three-month honeymoon phase, mebbe longer, until they discover their woman is not so perfect after all. They will then use the woman's imperfections — suddenly finding fault in everything she does and says — as the reason why they need to kick her to the curb. The alternative, for someone not addicted to the butterflies, is to stay with his bipolar Barbie come what may, because she *appears* perfect to him and the outside world. If she looks good on his arm, and is tolerable in most other ways, he will likely stay stuck in the lousy situation awhile longer.

Trophies sit on a shelf—pretty, yet lifelessly fading in luster and in need of constant dusting off. Eventually you get tired of looking at it, and it just blends into the background. That's not me, and hopefully never will be! Since I'm aging and most men seem to prefer younger women, I think I'm safe. No trophy wife here. As I've said, once the looks of youth fade, you'd better hope you've chosen a mate who is a great conversationalist! Otherwise, that trophy is just taking up space on your shelf, and you can't just throw it away. There's something to be said for being happy rather than just content.

He Loves Her, He Loves Me Not

This guy talked about his ex-girlfriend practically the entire time we were together. Not a coffee date, rather I'd made the mistake of planning a day with him in my neck of the woods. So not only was I a sounding board for him, I had to entertain him the entire day while listening to him talk about someone he was clearly still in love with who didn't want him. Not a smart way to start off with someone new. Colossal waste of my time! Even more so because I wasn't the least bit interested, but didn't have the heart to say as much. I suffered through the day needlessly because I felt he needed someone to listen.

Not. My. Problem! Coffee, ten minutes, and shut that noise down!

Bored Voyage!

I had dinner with this guy and just wasn't feeling it. He seemed all enthused himself though; said he was going on a cruise the following week, "Call you when I get back!" Whether he had a cruise or not, he didn't call after the week was up. Not that I cared in the least. Thing is, I was already onto the fact that this is a typical blow-off move — saying you're going on vacation but will be in touch when you return — and half expected I'd never hear from him again. *Vios con Dios!*

Yet another example of a man who didn't have the nerve to say he just wasn't into me, or mebbe he was but didn't follow through later for whatever reason. Either way, the bottom line was the same. *POOF!* Coward.

Merry Minstrel

We met for a cocktail and he laughed at everything I said. This was one of those times when I felt like I was on the clock, not just carrying the entire conversation but doing all the entertaining for the price of a drink (the gas to get there cost more). Mebbe he should pay me — time is money, and my professional entertainment ain't free!

When I announced I was leaving, he laughed.

Can't read minds, never know what people's personal hang-ups are. While I admired this man's jovial spirit, it was symptomatic of something else. A lousy communicator will be a lousy partner. Don't take it personally, be glad you dodged a bullet! Communication is SO important in a relationship!

Mr. Monopoly

We had agreed to meet at a public event where there were lots of other people—always a wise choice in case there is zero spark. Despite being fat, bald and missing a tooth, *he* was not attracted to *me*. He said we could be friends though. Two weeks later, he posted a pic on FB of his new girlfriend — adorably petite. Natch.

Two nice people who just weren't meant for each other. He has since married the little girl. Oh, I'm happy for him. Not everyone you meet is meant for you. I just resent the idea that some men, by nature, will be quick to dismiss a woman they are not instantly attracted to. Women seem to be far more forgiving of a man's physical appearance. He never even gave me a chance!

This got me thinking… Does it boil down to ego?

My friend Carl has a different view. He doesn't believe ego has anything to do with it. He says it's all just fear — a *fear of what others will think*. If you come to a party with a fat date, or a woman who's unattractive or taller than you, what will your friends think?! The right answer is, or should be, *true friends would give her a chance because she's important to you*, but that's not what happens in the mind of the man. If you choose not to take this fantastic woman to the party because you are afraid of what your "friends" will think, that says more about you than her, or even them. And that, Carl, is the ego at work!

Carl went on to say that we are genetically predispositioned to fear only two things: falling, and loud noises. Our fear of what others will think of our date is irrational then — something we've told ourselves over the years based on irrational, unnatural fear. Fight or flight then, what's a guy to do? Fight for her honor, or run before he even gets to know her?! There is a third choice though. Stand still. Bring her to the party, (assess the threat) see how it goes, because it's what's inside us that counts. Who cares if she's taller than you, overweight or otherwise unattractive to others? YOU are the one dating her! When you connect with amazing chemistry, you're the only two people in the room!

Added to this dilemma is the fact that men prefer younger women, a genetic predisposition to keep the species going. At my age, older men have seen the better part of their lives and are entering their twilight years, the winter of their lives. I'm entering the fall of mine, but look and feel summerish. Now what? Couple that with the fact that I'm still in my prime while most older men are slowing down sexually. I could easily argue the point that, if women statistically live longer than men, doesn't it stand to reason it's the women who should be dating younger men?! That's another argument, read on!

Whether you side with Carl's fear theory or mine on ego, the bottom line is the same — men care what others think about the appearance of the woman on their arm. Perhaps Carl and I are both right — a combination of ego and fear, or fear because of the erroneous voice in our head controlled by the ego.

My friend Chuck says, "The prettier they are, the more (trouble) work they are!" When you choose the prettiest woman in the room, you're likely unwittingly choosing the hottest mess.

The rest of us wallflowers are going home alone, despite your hanging belly and bald spot. I can hear you saying, "But I'm in good shape!" I, despite being overweight and middle-aged, can run circles around your petite princesses, your bi-polar bottle-blonde Barbies. At school, I fly past hyperventilating students on the staircases because I can, but you'd never know it to look at me. Know why? Because you can't judge a book by its cover! (Well, mebbe this one) You just don't know who a person is until you spend some time getting to know him or her. You want to really know someone? Spend a weekend away together! Now *there's* something that's broken up many a couple! But I digress...

The handsomest man in the room seeks out the prettiest woman in the room, believing he deserves this. Ironically, it is often times the handsomest people who are the most insecure! Read any psychology book; it's true! You would think they would have the utmost confidence, being so attractive, desired, put to-gether — seemingly the total package! But none of us is perfect. Who knows where the insecurity comes from. Fear of losing looks as they get older? Fear that people won't like what they see once they truly get to know you? (More irrational fears — we all get older) I don't know, but I accept that it is real. And I submit that if Mr. Handsome is insecure about who he is, perhaps finding a secure but somewhat less-attractive woman who is otherwise the total package might serve him better than the prettiest mess in the room.

I've heard you can manifest what you want into your life. I'd always thought the way to do this is to make a list of the things you want in a mate and ask the Universe to bring you a person with those qualities. When the time is right, it will happen. Carl says that's actually *not* how it works. When manifesting, the law of attraction suggests we thank the Universe for sending you the person you are meant to be with — *who is already here*, you just haven't met him/her yet. But your person is out there, waiting for the right time to be revealed. Carl added, *"You should also thank*

the Universe for the feeling of joy you will have when you meet him."
Sounds good to me!

Ask yourself, what kind of person do I habitually date? Thinking about those you've dated or been attracted to, what did they all have in common? Do you have a type? When I sat down to do this, I realized I'm a sucker for a big toothy smile. If a man has a beautiful broad smile, I get tunnel vision. That's what I'm most attracted to. However, if you look beyond attraction, really look at the person on the inside, feel the energy, the chemistry between the two of you, isn't that what's most important? If you didn't care what people thought about the person on your arm, you might be surprised who you find yourself dating! How is that old pattern working out for you? No good? Break the cycle — step outside your 'comfort' zone and try something different! Expand your horizons!

Like magnets, the handsomest of men seem to easily find the most beautiful women. I've come to learn that looks don't matter in the end. Even a not-so-handsome human can be a fine person and surprisingly great lover! My ex-husband was gorgeous (although I didn't think so when I first met him and gave him a chance), but it mattered not in the end.

Many a tear has to fall,
But it's all in the game.

Patriots Fanfan

"I don't know, what do you think?' OK, I've said it before —
If a guy wants to be with you, HE WILL BE! None of this wishy-
washy crap. All I hear is, "I dunno, I don't really want you. Still,
it's better than being alone…" No matter which side of the fence
his decision fell, I had already decided for him — we weren't a
match.

When I'm shopping for a pair of jeans, and I'm looking in
the mirror trying them on, I know right away if they're a good fit.
If I have to think about it, they're going back on the rack! NEXT!!

Vanilla Ice

Sometimes you meet someone who is somewhere in-between The One and "Nice, but not quite for me". That's where this man ranked. I could've easily fallen for him, but I sensed he was leaning more toward "Nice but…" (teehee, see what I did there?)

We'd met for appetizers at a pub offering trivia during a Patriots game, win/win for me! He was a sweet person, friendly enough, successful, had the *Three Tions…* At the end of the night he'd said he'd call, and I was hopeful he would. I am also very familiar with this lie, so I waited. After a week, it was clear he wouldn't be calling.

Normally, I'd let it go as I never chase. However, since he was 'liking' stuff on my FB page, I was a bit confused. Why call attention to yourself if you're pulling a Houdini?! So I called him out on it. I told him it was wrong to say he was going to call when he *knew* he wasn't going to. "Please be kind to the next woman!" I implored. He responded with, "I surely will!" <Hurt me> and indeed he was. FB, I hate you!!! He posts pics of all the fun times they have. She is younger, petite, adorable, living near him… all the things I am not (OK, mebbe I'm somewhat adorable). She also has a young child, which surely makes him feel like the hero/provider. Some men are all about that (She *NEEDS* me!). I can totally see them together, and that's a good thing. I'm happy for him, and he continues to 'like' my stuff so we're technically still 'friends'.

You already know how I feel about exchanging FB friend requests, and I wonder if I made a mistake doing the FB thing with him. While he's harmless, seeing him so happy while I'm still alone is somehow selfishly hard to do, even though I know in my heart of hearts that he was not The One. In taking care of self, I don't enjoy feeling sad, as these posts sometimes leave me. I'm not the jealous type, thank the gods. Jealousy is so unbecoming as it reeks of insecurity. However, if seeing someone's posts bothers you enough, it's not a bad idea to 'unfollow' him/her, remove the person from your friends list, or even block him/her if s/he is active on your wall — serving as a constant reminder — at least until you are in a better place emotionally. FYI, until you friend someone, s/he isn't supposed to be able to find you on FB via just your cell phone number (or see things on your wall) if your privacy settings are tight enough! Food for thought. Keep your security settings high, and hide that phone number in your FB profile!

Barely Needed

So romantic, all the excuses why we couldn't meet each time a day was chosen. (Cue the music: Coming in, and out of your life…) The best excuse was, at the 12th hour, "Even though my evil, bipolar wife left two years ago, the divorce still isn't final." Folks, that's a red flag flapping furiously right there. See it?

By the way, just an observation: Many men have told me their ex-wife was "crazy bipolar". OK, men need to feel needed, I get it. But was it in their best interest to choose a life partner who was unstable? Was she medicated before but not now? I don't get it. You marry a woman with the potential to make your life a full-screen drama, then get mad at all of womankind when she snaps. Newsflash! We're not all evil! Still, if she snapped her fingers today and said she wanted him back, he'd prolly run to her!

Anyhoo, about two months later, this guy sent a familiar romantic text to me that was clearly intended for someone else. *Oops!* Liars abound. (If a person wants to be with you…) I've had a slew of those.

Here's the lesson, folks. Games will be played. *Trust your gut!* Listen, *really listen to it,* and it will never deceive you the way some of these potential suitors will.

And if he's badmouthing his ex…

Argumentative Guy

We've all met someone like this throughout our lifetime — the kind of person who finds fault in every little thing you say. You are always wrong, no matter what, and even the simplest comments result in an argument. It gets to the point where I'll sit there quietly, but the arguer will ask me questions to make the painful conversation go on, and on... I always start out nice, but then the irritation builds, and I'll either shut them down with a good argument on my end, or I'll excuse myself altogether. It's not that I can't argue every little point, it's that *I don't want to!* Why bother? This is entertaining?? Life is full of enough hate and angry negativity, why spoil an otherwise good time spewing toxic waste?! Not fun!

We had a mutual friend, which can sometimes make things awkward as you JUST KNOW s/he's going to go back and compare notes with said friend later, especially if the date was a bust. I knew enough to keep my mouth shut; I let him spew his crap and then we said our goodbyes. He gave me a hug but I knew it meant nothing.

Later that night, much later, he called (from his bed) to see if I'd gotten home safely. Huh? I said I did — a while ago — and he asked why I sounded so surprised to hear from him. I told him honestly that he'd departed quickly after he said, 'Nice meeting you', which is the polite blow-off phrase akin to 'Hava nice life!', and he told me that was negative thinking. (It's time for bed and he's STILL looking for an argument) "Are you a mind reader?

176

How could you possibly know if I was going to call you again or not?!"

Exactly. Jerk! And then they wonder why they're divorced!! If you can't communicate effectively, no relationship will work out, romantic or otherwise.

Of all the very many dates I've been on over the years (well over a hundred!), I can only think of two people I actually connected with and was truly excited about. We want what we want. Sometimes, what we want is bad for us. We think with the heart instead of the head (and most men think with the head with the hole in it). Some say this is OK, as the heart knows what it needs to be happy. There's a Spanish saying, *"Without madness, there is no love."* When you love someone, s/he can drive you insane! But that's what creates the passion we so crave. As I get older, I still want passion, but I also crave quiet. I don't want to argue with my mate; I want my home to be a harmonious sanctuary I look forward to retreating to. Using the head is wise, but just because someone looks good on paper doesn't mean s/he's *right* for you. ("There are a lot of nice guys in the world, you don't have to marry them all!") IF s/he's got the *Three Tions*, and IF s/he makes your heart go pitter patter, you know you're onto something! If the occasional argument is passionate and deserved, s/he's a keeper!

To calmly argue a point is not the same as being argumentative. Good riddance!

Chatty Caddy

When we felt comfortable enough to exchange phone numbers, we talked for literally 35 minutes. I use the word 'we' loosely. He talked. The whole. Entire. Time. I even put the phone down a couple of times and walked away for five minutes each time. He didn't even pause for the occasional, "You know?" to see if I was still breathing!! At the 35-minute mark — which never should've happened (bail at the 11-minute mark as a general rule!) — I told him I'd been listening for 35 minutes and just couldn't take another minute longer. He laughed, said nice talking (at) to you, have a good night. A few days later, as if everything were hunky dory, he texted to say he thinks we have a lot in common. Like how would he know?!

Folks, your time is precious. I know this, but it seemed like he needed a shoulder or something. I let him babble because I still got to enjoy my TV show knowing he wasn't about to pause for me to talk at all. Eventually, it did become a nuisance for me as, c'mon, how long does he really think this can go on anyway? Oh, he *knows* what he's doing; of course he does! But here's a guy who'd been divorced twice already. I'm thinking communication issues... My point here is, don't waste time on someone who clearly doesn't care what you have to say! Someone truly interested in you is fully engaged in the conversation. There are two of us here!

Choo Choo Charley

I was riding a train into NY City to see Barbra Streisand perform, and stopped at the food car for a sandwich and drink. While watching the server gather my things, I was trying to remember the name of a Saturday Night Live player and made conversation with him by blurting, "Who is Church Lady? His real name?" He thought for half a second and said, "Oh, Dana Carvey!" I lit up, "That's it!!" We wished each other well and I went on my merry way back to my seat.

About a month later… Yeah. Turns out he was local. He answered my ad and we talked on the phone. He informed me he worked as a train conductor — specifically in the food car. Bells and whistles went off in my head and I suddenly blurted, "Who is Church Lady?" He gasped, said he remembered me, wished he'd gotten my phone number on the train — and firmly believed this was kismet! Fate in motion!

We went on a nice date and agreed to see each other again. Since he was only available Tuesday nights, I became his Tuesday night thing to do. He was a very quiet man, and so I inexorably had to carry the conversations (and by now you know how I feel about *that!*). Each Tuesday, we would go to the restaurant of my choice, have a nice meal, and say goodbye with a quick kiss in his car. Ever the gentleman, he never pressed for deeper kisses or more. OK, there might've been *one* attempt on his part. I'm not too sure. One night, while giving me the goodnight kiss, he opened his mouth to cavernous proportions. That's it. Nothing emerged. Odd (kinda like the shape of his head. As my friend Erin would say, "I can't get with that!"). It never happened again. But I digress...

After about six weeks of this, my birthday came around. He took me to Boston to see Phantom of the Opera after a terrific meal that Sunday night. I was very impressed as I knew this wasn't cheap. However, we sat in the upper-nosebleed section and I could not have seen the stage past the bobblehead in front of me even if we'd sat closer. At the end of the evening, I gave him the usual quick peck and he asked if we were on for Tuesday...

The following day, I received a beautiful bouquet of flowers. The card attached read simply, 'Happy Birthday. Charley'.

Funny thing about that is, he prolly thought I didn't know his last name and purposely omitted it. He was fishing. It must've driven him crazy that I didn't care enough to ask or something. I've mentioned I live in a small state? Yeah, well he'd told me his mom worked for a certain chain, my cousin was a manager for said chain. Together we figured out who his mom was, and I deduced they must have the same surname. He must've thought it odd that I hadn't asked after seven weeks of dating, but it was actually *he* who never learned *my* last name! (that I know of...)

When Tuesday night came around, we had a nice meal — except this time I decided he'd do the talking! If things didn't go well, I'd release him, as it didn't seem fair to keep this locomotive going at a dying crawl. After our silent dinner, on the drive home he asked, "Are you always this quiet?" HUH?!? *GRRRRRR!!!* I explained to him that I felt like I always did the talking here and wanted to give *him* a chance. He came back with, "I know I'm quiet, I just wondered if you are!" (Dafuq? Remember all those conversations I carried??!) So when we arrived at my place, and he asked if we were on for the following Tuesday, I dropped the ax. He was a very sweet man and deserved more. Me too. I loved being treated so well, but things weren't progressing and it wasn't fair to either of us to keep an immobile car on the tracks.

Moving forward. Several weeks later, I was driving into work at about 5am and stopped at a red light. There he was, right next to me at the same light. Like what are the chances?!! I could see out of the corner of my eye, his laser beams burning a hole in me as he leaned over to magically draw my attention. I wasn't having it. Determined *not* to let him think we truly were star-crossed lovers, I toyed with the buttons on my radio to seem engrossed, and floored it in warp-speed reaction time as soon as the light turned green. His Neon was no match for my Monte Carlo, even if he didn't drive like Grandma Moses, and I left him eating my dust once again. <Sigh> I hope he found love, I really do.

I've long felt if your paths cross more than once, that's no mistake! It's fate putting you together bow that the time is right. Charley and I were definitely not a match though. I've no idea why fate kept throwing us together, but you can't run an electric train without a spark.

I've heard guys snap that "Women don't give Average Joe a chance!" Like Dad said, "There are a lot of nice guys in the world, you don't have to…" There's nothing wrong with Average Joe, he makes a great partner! However, since I am anything but average, call me shallow but I would not be happy with him. Average Joe needs to give Plain Jane a chance! Average women need love too. *No no no, it ain't me, babe!*

We Got a Runner!

This guy claimed to have money and posted pictures of "his" gorgeous home to prove it. Showing off your tangible assets (not muscles, but cars, boats, etc. OK, showing off your muscles is arrogant too.) is always a red flag: "Here's what I own", not who I am. And how do you know they actually own this stuff? Lies abound. He sounded decent enough though, so I gave it a shot.

He chose a place near him for us to meet. It didn't look half bad from the outside. This bar, unbeknownst to me but made clear by him once I sat, was a well-known biker establishment (not that there's anything wrong with that but) where you could get any drug of choice. Charming. He then began to criticize everyone and everything about the place as he finished his beer. Clearly he was (mentally ill) in a hurry — dropped $3 on the bar and abruptly ran off. It took me a few seconds to process what had just happened, and when the smiling bartender came over with the bill, it all started to come together for me. The cheapo had stuck me with a portion of his bill, as the bartender naturally figured we were together. It wasn't enough to bother the bartender with (Not her fault, although she shouldn't have assumed anything) but enough to ruin my mood. *GRRRRRRR!*

So what's the answer? Establish separate checks right away when the bartender comes for your order? Pay for your drink as soon as it's delivered to get that message across? You just never know if the man will pay on the first meeting (it's not a bad idea to have that conversation beforehand), but I couldn't have known he'd stick me with *his* drink. While what he did was slightly better than "I forgot my wallet," it was still a low move on his part. It happens. Dad always said *have cash on hand — be ready for anything!*

The red flags were there but I stoopidly chose to ignore them. It's not typical for a guy to have me do the drive, let alone take me to a "classy" place and stiff the server. Just sayin'. Agree to meet no more than half-way, and research the venue if it's unfamiliar!

Boston Marathoner

Met a guy at an Annie Leibowitz photo display in Boston. We walked through in a mere 10 minutes, so decided to grab a quick bite to fill some time. My Boston guy looked so bored. How dare he! I am anything but boring! I don't know why I did it, but with nothing to lose I decided to have a little fun with him. Since I had to carry the conversation, I started the next sentence with, "My therapist says..." After that, he couldn't get out of there fast enough! He actually *ran* from me! It was so worth the laugh. And I'm sure he's still telling *that* story!

Did I have to carry the conversation because *he* was boring, or because he was bored with me? Why bother reading into it, the bottom line is the same — he just wasn't attracted. Again, women are so much more willing to look past the physical and make a connection. Can't fight Mother Nature. I wasn't proud of myself, but I also needed to walk away with my ego intact. My point is, if the attraction isn't there, nothing you do is going to win him over—not if there's no second date. I wasn't going to change his mind by wishing him well, but we might've ended on a good note if he had behaved better. It would've been the classier thing for me to do — call it a day and wish him well — but I was calling him out in my own humorous way and using that as a survival tactic. The way he was treating me was not acceptable. I'm a survivor — I changed the dynamics to something I could live with. You want to go home with your head held high!

Gym Addict

He was a decent guy with a small appetite. He'd confessed he liked women younger (than myself, even though he was older) and thinner, as he doesn't eat much (Neither do I, but whatever. I know I look like I can pack it in if I want to). He made it a point to go to the gym every day, and see his daughter nearly every night. That's great, but when I asked him if he really thought he had time to squeeze a woman into his life, he just smiled and shrugged. (Where's the exit??) I've said it and said it again — If a person wants to be with you, s/he will be! It's up to that person to make time in his/her busy schedule to include you. If this can't be done, that person is not ready for a relationship. Unless you're just looking for casual dating, *sayonara!*

Not sure why he indicated in his profile he's looking for a long-term relationship as he clearly has very little free time. We left it that we could hang out as friends, as we were both musicians who enjoyed supporting local bands but didn't enjoy sitting alone. We agreed to meet at a certain club to see a certain band on a certain night. When the night came, he was running late… Because I had been talking to my cousin about it, I sent her a funny text about him, except I accidentally sent it to him. Yeah. He never called again.

The lesson here? If you're going to be catty, make sure you double check the name of the person you're sending the message to. He may not have time for you, but he likely makes time to read his messages. 'Nuff said.

Lora's Losers

Many moons ago, my cousin had a dinner date with a guy who "forgot" his wallet at home... Naturally, she paid the bill, never heard from the guy again, and felt lousy for a while afterward. We had a feeling this was a game of his, and she was not his first victim. So when he answered my ad, the wheels started turning. Lora dared me to accept the date and excuse myself just before the bill came, give the guy a taste of his own medicine. Not one to turn down a dare in my youth, and knowing this guy needed to be taught a lesson (I'm fiercely protective of those I love), I toyed with the idea. In full disclosure, I let him know who I was (Dumb! If you're going to plot something evil you don't go and divulge too much info!). He said it was rotten luck he'd forgotten his wallet (HAHAHAHA!), and while he unfortunately didn't hit it off with Lora, that doesn't mean we shouldn't meet and explore where this could go.

I agreed to a date, got all dolled up and went to meet him. Guess what? He didn't show. Joke's on me. That's what I get for playing stoopid dating games! I should have left it alone and let karma get him. What can I say, I was young. Won't happen again! Not by me, anyway. I'm sure wherever he is, some resourceful wench has taught him a valuable lesson by now.

Seems no matter how mentally prepared you are for this to happen, in the end you can still get stiffed — lest you stiff the server instead. Happened to me once too (See Cute Construction

Connie). For a long time afterward, I had this fantasy of being prepared to flee the exact moment a guy tells me he's forgotten his wallet. Can't get blamed for stiffing the waitress if HE is the one left holding the bill. He's likely got cash in his pocket. Throw your half on the table and run!

Meet for coffee!

Lora told me about another date she had in which she arrived to find her target much shorter than stated, toothless, wearing "hick" clothing — and accompanied by four similar friends! It was like a cult following. I asked her, "So what's the deal? You date the one, you get the other five as a bonus?" Mebbe they were completely harmless, but can you imagine how a woman by herself might feel walking into that situation? Bizarre! "Scariest group of freaks I've ever seen!" said she.

Yeah, I got nothin'. I've never seen it before or since. If you encounter anything this bizarre, *RUN!!* Don't put yourself in an uncomfortable or unsafe position — ever — if you can help it!! Apparently, another woman had put up a warning about them; good for her!! Report that noise!!

Sow Vain

This guy was full of himself. Know how you can tell? When they don't STFU about themselves! Don't *tell* me how wonderful you are, *show* me! Actions really do speak louder than words! I had to hear about how he's written three books (yawners, no doubt), had his own business (once), lives in a nice house in a nice neighborhood (I work there, it's OK). He also thought he was *all that* physically, but let's just say the better part of his years were behind him in that respect.

We agreed to meet at a nice club where a friend's jazz band would be playing, other friends of mine joining. I recognized him instantly and went right over to him at the bar. The snooty look on his face told me instantly he was not the least bit attracted and his wall went waaaay up. He had a drink in front of him and asked me if he should hail the bartender so I could get myself a drink (Class act. I'm sure that's what he tells himself). I declined, and then he said, "You can go hang with your friends, don't let me stop you!" UGH!

Lesson here?? He didn't have to dismiss me twice; I was out of there in a shot. But what gets me is, *I'd* invited *him* to join us if he wanted, and when he saw a pretty friend of mine he wanted, I had to watch him schmooze with her all night (although she was clearly not interested, just polite). And he joined our group, so that I continue to have to see him whenever we get together as a group. We avoid each other, which is a shame, as that's not what polite people do, but we have no control over the shallow actions of others. He was yet another older man who thought he could get someone younger than me. Can't blame a guy for trying? I actually enjoy watching him work a crowd of ladies, getting shot down time after time. Just because someone smiles at you in conversation doesn't mean s/he is truly interested. When they are, you will know it!

This guy was (and still is) rather arrogant. While arrogance in small doses and done right can be sexy, there was nothing sexy about him. A woman would have to be a bit under confident herself, methinks, to want a man like this. After all, arrogance is a sign of insecurity at its core. Arrogant people also seem angry to me, which is never good. Angry intimidation can make a weaker woman do things she will resent. Women are typically more eager to please, willing to put their own needs aside to make things work, then later become resentful that they were the only one to make concessions. And what you allow will continue. It's not good to lose your identity. The idea, then, is to go about your business doing what you love, and hopefully you will find someone with similar interests. Changing who you are is going to be disappointing and temporary when the sizzle starts to fizzle. Hold out for the right partner—preferably someone who is not arrogant and angry, but sincere and healthy.

Kemosabe Wannabe

I'm not typically attracted to dark men or blondes, but I wouldn't discount either if I thought we had enough in common otherwise. So when a Black man claiming to be a Native American chatted intelligently with me and asked me out, I was intrigued.

This was many years ago when biracial couplings were still rare in the northeast, so it didn't help matters that he was decked out in a 10-gallon cowboy hat and draped in large pieces of 'Indian' jewelry (also rare in New England despite our Native American populations). I told myself I didn't care that people were staring, but truth be told I was not comfortable with all the attention we were getting.

Not visible in his online photo were long, thin braids in back that added to the "Where is this cat *from*?!" mystique. Clearly he was hiding a chrome dome under that hat, and mebbe had some other secrets I'd find out about soon enough. I found myself tempted to quip, "I can still see the barcode on your weave!" *What'cha hidin'?*

Not wanting to feel shallow, I told myself looks don't matter, and he can play Cowboys & Indians if he wants — it's what's inside that counts. He was nice. So nice, in fact, that he confided he was legally married. "We're separated, still living together just for financial reasons. I wear the ring out of respect for her." Native American on his great-great-grandmother's side (Four generations back. So that's about 6% Native American? Pretty sure that doesn't qualify him for any benefits). Oh, and "jobless at the moment. It's hard finding a job when you're dyslexic. I can pay my half of the bill but you'll have to cover the tip."

OK, I understand why he played it this way. If he'd told me all this upfront, I likely wouldn't have come out to meet him. He's right (not the dyslexia thing; everything combined). But what did he think was going to happen when I found out all this — especially the fact that he was legally married?! HELLOOOOO, YOU'RE IN NO POSITION TO BE DATING!!

Folks, people are going to find out! The omission of truth is deceitful, and might as well be considered a lie. It's not fun to be robbed of your free will — the greatest thing separating us from the rest of the animals. *So who do… Who do ya think you're fooling?* Only yourself. Yes, put your best foot forward, but *give people the info they need to know when they are deciding whether or not you are right for them.* Otherwise, you may become a very malcontent serial dater. That can get expensive for a jobless person.

Desperado

I recently asked a friend how she made out with a date she was to have gone on the previous Saturday night. She said he'd cancelled last-minute because his mom was rushed to the emergency room. I burst out laughing and said, "Oh c'mon, don't you know that's the oldest trick in the book?" I proceeded to tell her about a date I'd had, drinks at a country line-dancing style club, when — exactly at 9pm — his phone pinged and he flatly said (bad actor), "Oh no. My mom was rushed to the hospital. I've got to go." He didn't live nearby, so I told him he'd better drive really fast. "Hope your MOM will be OK!"

My friend assured me that it had to be true because he'd texted her late that night to update her. That, ladies and gentlemen, was him putting her on the back burner — after he didn't make out so well on the date he actually went on! I'd bet my next paycheck on it. Games are played, this is one of them, (Having a friend call you so you can pretend there's some emergency if you want to bail), and it's amazing to me how many people buy into it. We are trusting souls by nature, until we've graduated from the School of Hard Knocks.

Red Scare

I was not attracted to his nickel teeth, apparently something popular in Russia when he was growing up there. He'd admitted he was still in love with a woman he'd dated from the ads, that she'd moved an hour north to get away from him (yes, he admitted this too!) and that the distance had not dissuaded him from driving past her house every. Single. Night. Sometimes twice in one day! "She has called the cops on me, and there's a restraining order, but I just have to go every night." Too bad, so sad, *gotta go!*

There are red flags waving, and then there are CODE RED ALERTS!! I hope I don't have to spell out why this guy would NOT be a good candidate for any self-respecting woman. There's no help for this one.

So many of these men need a mommy. Sorry, guys, but the next time I change diapers, it will be for my grandchild. No rush there either.

Christine's Stories

Several of my dearest friends have had nightmarish ad dates of their own. Chris allowed me to share a couple of her most memorable. She had just gotten divorced after many years of marriage, and was a bit out of the loop on how the dating games are now played. She agreed to meet a guy at the movies. He tugged hard on her hair, to be playful. I guess. Being the sweet person she is, she just smiled and let it go, but she was scared (red flag waving!!). Then the guy blew in her face two times during the movie. WTH? The first time she felt the breeze, she was hoping it was just an air vent and ignored it. The second time, sure it was him, she was thoroughly grossed out. She looked over at him, and he was smiling back at her. Ugh. What was he thinking?? Turn-*off!* (Reminds me of the time a guy barked in my face during a party date among coworkers. Like why would anyone think that's sexy? 'Bob Barker' was not granted a second date!) Then, he tossed his jacket over his lap and kept drawing her hand to it. Yeah. She excused herself to the bathroom — and left the theater! Good girl. Take no crap!

I've said earlier don't go to a movie on a first date as it's too noisy in a theater. Don't go to a movie on the second date either. It's too dark, too easy for a guy to get to second base, unless of course that's what you want. (Why do I feel dirty all of a sudden, like I just gave creepers a helpful hint?)

On a second date with someone else that she actually clicked with, Chris was sitting at the bar with her date on one side, and his friend on the other. Got a feeling where this is going? Yeah, she got a feeling — the friend's hand on her thigh! Said 'friend' then slipped her his phone number. Although she kept all this quiet from her date, he never called again. Who knows why people disappear, but honestly? Ninety-nine out of a hundred times, it's not you. Something else was going on in their lives that you weren't privy to. Easier said than done, I know, but don't take it to heart! Bottom line, they are not available, and therefore not a good catch. Bye!

On some personal advice here, I would say Chris was trying a fill a void in her life, trying to find love again after her divorce (Aren't we all?). I've learned, though, that when you break off a relationship, you need some regrouping time. Allow yourself the opportunity to get back to *you*. Sit back with your hurt feelings and see what lessons need to be learned, instead of trying to replace the hurt with new love. While those happy butterflies in your tummy sure do feel good — and make for a sweet distraction — you're really not in a good place after a breakup to give yourself to someone else. Let the healing begin; learn and grow. Then, when the time is right, the Universe will give you what you need next. I love the attentive idea of having somebody checking in every day and texting, but then you meet and it's hardly ever what you expected anyway. Online dating can create a perpetual roller coaster of emotions, and you don't need that when you're trying to heal.

Touchy Touchy!

This man had seen that I'd checked out his profile, and politely thanked me for doing so. Nice opener! His ad mentioned how life is short and so it should be filled with laughter. I can do that; I'm kinda funny. So I tried to be funny. Mostly it worked; I'd hooked him in, but then I made a fatal error. I corrected his spelling. He knew my name before I told it to him, so I asked if it appeared in my ad. He said yes, so I went in and fixed that. No sense in putting too much personal info out there until you've screened these people. Although I hadn't thanked him, he responded with, "Your welcome." See the misspelling? To that I responded, YOU'RE welcome! ☺ Well he didn't like that, I guess, because his next line was, "Good luck fishing." Oooooookaaaaaaay then!

Put your best foot forward. I've said this before, but I'll go a step further. In this case, I unwittingly attacked his fragile male ego. How dare I correct his spelling! His ad had mentioned he wants a nonjudgmental woman. Why wasn't I listening? To correct his spelling could be taken to mean I'd judged his smarts (even though he corrected me first), and would likely keep doing it. No doubt his last woman trashed his ego and now he can't take any more of that. Really, I was just being cute, but he wasn't thinking of things from my editor/comedian perspective. It was a lesson for me, though, when he blew me off: LISTEN! He came right out and said he didn't like judgment, and I should've caught that. Never never never smash the male ego upon first contact!! Anyway, it never would've worked if he's *that* sensitive. I want someone I can tease back and forth with, so if he can't (grow some testosterone) handle my brand of humor… NEXT!!

Beer Bear

Nice man, I'll say that. And I had a feeling, when I saw one solitary pic of just his face, that he might be a big boy, despite his Body Type description of "a few extra pounds". But you know what? My ad read the same way, and I'm fit, so I try not to judge that way. Well he was nearly as wide as he was tall, and he was TALL! He was also missing a tooth or three, but who's counting. OK, sorry to sound shallow here, but you know how I feel about this. If you don't mind all this, fine, but you might be better suited to another toothless smoker/drinker, just sayin'. Someone who is health — and appearance — conscious is likely looking for the same. I try my best to take care of myself and expect the same in a partner. Not perfect, but attentive to self. I'd like to be someone's wife, not a widow.

We talked for five hours. I didn't expect this would be the case when we first sat down together. He was a sweet man who, like me, needed a break in the love department. In the end, though, I decided he wasn't a match for several different reasons. He was a homebody; I like to go out and enjoy various interests. He wasn't looking to be married but wanted a live-in companion, whereas I have my own home and won't sell it without a major commitment. He prefers a slow, short stroll in the woods to my seven-mile, moderately-paced hikes in the hills. He kept farmers' hours, and I'm a night owl. We just weren't on the same page for the things that really matter, despite our fluid conversation.

200

While it's important to have your own interests, friends and space, you really need to find someone who is headed in the same direction and enjoys some of the things you do.

Also, he was very gruff with his hands (and they were rough to the touch since he was a carpenter). Occasionally, to make a point, he would pound the table. The table would shake, and then so would I! Scared the heck out of me more than once! The guy prolly wasn't even aware he was doing it, and all the while I was taking mental notes on how there's no way in hell this man could possibly be a tender lover if he's like a bull in a China shop.

♥

When it's right, you'll know it. 'Nuff said?

Lonesome Loser

We were already off to a bad start when, during a miscommunication, we ended up going to different restaurants for our meeting. I knew I should have kept it simple, a coffee. You know it's going to be one of those sounding board nights if he's so eager to buy you dinner instead of meeting for a coffee. They frame it like they want to be a gentleman, "We can enjoy each other's company even if we don't hit it off romantically." In the end, you sit there for three hours, as I did, listening to him talk about his two ex-wives and his rather recent ex-girlfriend, blah blah blah.

This happened once before, where there was a miscommunication and I ended up at a different restaurant than my date, however, *that* man was a gentleman and told me to stay where I was — he would come to me. But Lonesome Loser? Not so gentlemanly. I'd called him from the restaurant I was at and he said, "I'm already here, you should come to me." I had suggested Italian and that's where I went, but he was at a Chinese restaurant because that's what he preferred. So that's what we did. Red flag waving on selfish stubbornness, and mebbe part of the reason why he's alone.

He also didn't look like his photos, obviously older than represented. He seemed to be missing his bottom teeth. Proceeded to tell me, again, that he'd had colorectal cancer and is missing his colon and rectum. Actually a cool procedure, where they rebuilt his rectum (great dinner conversation, eh!) from intestines. But I digress... He also had two shoulder replacements and two knee replacements, three strokes, two heart attacks, and something else I can't remember now. Perhaps a partial lobotomy. Methinks this guy has more than nine lives... Still, I watched in horror as he sucked down his scorpion bowl and proceeded to dump tons of salt on his MSG-laden sodium-rich Chinese food. All this as he retold how he'd broken some record at one of those all-you-can-eat buffets and gotten thrown out, too overloaded to even drive after that. Like how the hell has this guy not decided he's already exhausted eight of his nine lives and to make better choices? If I were a gold digger, he'd be perfect for me!

When he wasn't regaling me with stories of his exes and health problems, I heard about his sordid youth. How he could get chow mein sandwiches for five cents and then go drink all night with his buddies, overtaking the local Chinese restaurant. Extending their straws to reach over into the ladies' scorpion bowls without their knowledge. How the wait staffers were too afraid to kick them out even though they'd overstayed their welcome each time. Funny.

When you have nothing else going for you, discuss your assets... I heard all night about how much money he makes from his disability insurance (I'm sure that will help with the dialysis), has a big huge house, eight cars, blah blah blah. What was he thinking? What am I supposed to do with that information? Whoever latches her fingers into him won't have to live with his cavalier mouth for long. He's apparently got a lot of money to leave his kids when he exhausts his ninth life, somewhere around next year. I can only assume it made him feel like a big man, the provider.

Don't get me wrong, it's not that I can't be compassionate, but I am looking for a life partner here — someone who still has a good fifteen or twenty years to give me. He'd admitted he was a snorer. Smoked medical marijuana for his pain, looked high as a kite. Trouble keeping his wives. I can just hear him at his next wedding, taking his vows, *"I do! And I mean it this time!!"* Tell me again why you're such a great catch? Why would you tell me all this on the first date?! It's like you *want* me to run!

I was in my own car, and should have dipped out sooner, but it's very difficult when a man is paying for dinner and you're trying to leave as soon as you take your last bite. I tolerated the intolerable conversation and kept giving subtle hints such as looking at my phone for the time, putting my coat on, etc. but he wasn't budging. In the end, the server came back to ask if we needed anything else and I said no thanks, we're leaving! To that I stood, grabbing my doggy bag as he watched idly.

He walked me to my car, but I won't say that makes him a gentleman. The filth pouring from his mouth during our dinner pretty much indicated *that* hours before. How a man can behave so shamelessly upon first meeting is beyond me. He seemed like a classy gentleman in texts and over the phone, looked nice in his photos, but he dressed for me like he was attending a barn cleanup. All night I'd kept trying to find one redeeming quality. Alas…

He kept bragging about being a great kisser. (Beware the braggarts!) Who wants to kiss someone missing half his teeth? I'd already said my goodbyes at that point, doing nothing to emasculate him, and didn't stick around long enough to find out whether he was a good kisser or not.

I'm sure there was room in that big mouth for more than just two tongues. Wouldn't want to be the one to cause him to stroke out though. *"Have you heard about the lonesome loser? He's a loser but he still keeps on tryin'."* ~*Little River Band*

Ramblin' Man

This man had plans to move to CA to be with his son, so why start something here you can't finish? He was lonely, I get it, but the bags were practically packed. He was a true Ramblin' Man, just like the song says. Interesting man to say the least, and he claimed to be even more handsome than his pics, which didn't hurt. I was intrigued by the traveling artiste thing and was excited to meet him. Surely this was a man with some engrossing stories!

He was indeed handsome — for his age — but clearly he'd used older photos from when he was buff. He was now very skinny, which isn't a problem normally but it was misleading within the ad. He looked sickly. There are worse things in life, so I let that go, and we went hiking after our coffee meeting. The terrain wasn't bad at all, but still he was huffing and puffing as we walked. This is not a good sign, as clearly he's unfit if nothing else. Perhaps he had a history of smoking, drinking, whatever. This was the second red flag.

He finally admitted he was just looking for a local friend, if nothing else, just for now since he was moving sooner rather than later. I did call to see if he wanted to hike another time, as he had a free schedule and I can always use a new interesting friend, but he wasn't available and we never communicated again. I hope he's making beautiful copper jewelry in southern Cali, teaching his eager son the trade.

I need to thank him for teaching me the power of really listening. Women tend to let those little details get by, thinking 'If I'm special enough, he ain't goin' anywhere!' Not so. Mebbe if the attraction were amazing, we'd end up in Cali together one day, but nah. I believe, in the spirit of reason/season/lifetime. I came into his life briefly to teach him some lesson, perhaps one in moving to be with his family as he wasn't happy here. Sometimes, hearing something from a stranger makes things so much clearer.

Handy Dandy

There are times when you have a feeling the person isn't right for you, but s/he is so nice you know you should at least give it a try. HD was just such a person, and so after our coffee meet I decided to accept a date. He bragged he was handy with cars and home repairs, but that's not why I dubbed him thusly.

We went to Newport on his smoker motorcycle, not really comfy but a fun summer day thing to do. You can't really chat on a loud motorcycle though, so we were short on conversation while large on ocean views. We enjoyed a seafood lunch overlooking the water, and had a chance to chat then. Meh.

Once back at his place, I got the tour of his simple DIY home and met his daughter. She was a seemingly sweet kid in her early 20s who let him know she thought I was a good catch for him. This pleased him greatly. For whatever reason, he then started spouting all these wonderfully supportive words of wisdom, such as "Never stop dreaming! ... Never forget how special you are!" as though he (were talking to a mirror) felt I needed to hear all this stuff. Gee, thanks for the Stuart Smalley affirmations but *I got this!*

He then asked me to accompany him to an employee cookout, to which I asked if I could get back to him. I knew I had a conflict with my daughter's Girl Scout plans and she must come first. He seemed to understand. However, when I got back to him a week later that I was now free to join him, he responded with,

207

"My daughter feels I shouldn't see you any longer. You would be bad for me. (HUH??) I wish you all the luck in the world. Never give up on love! Reach for the stars! Blah blah blah…"

Um, so you're taking relationship advice from your kid, who has been with all of *two* "men" her entire life — one of which she nearly killed herself over? The same kid for whom you need to lock your bedroom door because she would steal from you for drug money? Tell me again why I'd be bad for you?!

OK, I did not say those things to him, I only thought them. Clearly the man had self-esteem issues and his addict (notorious liars!) daughter convinced him I'd been lying about my availability for this cookout. She sure seemed to like me enough before that.

I did not try to salvage whatever this was. I pulled up my bootstraps and somehow found the courage to get on with my wretched life. I hope, wherever he is now, that he's filled with gumdrops and glitter! That every day is rainbows, sunshine and lollipops! You are unique, you are fabulous, and doggonit, people like you! Don't you let anyone tell you otherwise! It's just you and your Jack Handy tonight, pal!! A plague upon your house! While you're riding your ^%$#& unicorn, be careful not to get the horn stuck up yer arse!

Doubt can be a scary thing. My father used to (half) jokingly ask me if I knew the difference between *faith* and *knowledge*. He would answer for me, "Faith is, I *believe* you are my daughter!" There was a time when I wondered about that myself, at least until I discovered the mole on my left cheek. I realized Dad had the same exact mole in the same exact spot — just as his older sister had. The family mole, huzzah! Hate it all you like; it's a treasure to me.

I had doubts, but faith is a much more powerful tool in your relationships. Occasional doubts are normal with your significant other. The real relationship begins after your first major disappointment. What both partners choose to do in light of those doubts can make or break the relationship.

We're told Noah built an ark to save (his family) the world before a great flood. He never doubted his belief. He brought aboard all these different animals, two by two — a male and female of each species. They floated on flooded earth for a year and 10 days. Ever wonder how many species went extinct during that boring, landless voyage?! If there's a moral to this one, it's that *people have their own dysfunctions and it's not your problem.* If your doubts firmly indicate the ship is sinking, bail before things start to really go down!

Snow flake

He said I should do the drive because he was paying for dinner. Still ignoring red flags at this stage of the game, like a dutiful idiot I complied. I guess this paying power made him feel like less of a schmuck somehow. At the restaurant, he checked his look in every mirror, very sure of his appearance (Even though he wasn't all that. Unsure?). In retrospect, I might have taken that as a sign...

We did have a nice dinner, good conversation, and so I wasn't surprised when he asked me for a second date. We sat in his car for a bit as it was a bitter cold night and we wanted to plan our next date, say a proper goodbye (dumb on my part all the same). We had fun, until we didn't. We'd kissed a little, and my hand fell to his chest pocket. I heard a crinkle, and like a curious little kitty, I reached in and grabbed its contents. I was holding a packet of cocaine. He was instantly outraged, yelling at me for invading his privacy or something like that. I was equally en-raged, reminding him we had agreed neither one of us does drugs! He then whined, "You don't know what a tough life I've had! Blah blah blah..."

If you're looking for pity, you'll find it in the dictionary between paranoid parasite and puke pustule! NEXT!!!

Garrulous Garry

As you know, I prefer to talk to people on the phone before meeting. You can usually get a good sense of who they are before deciding if you'd like to meet. Garry did all the talking, and he'd asked me what other dating sites he could try. Hello? Are we to be just friends? Texting buddies?? Careful what you put out there!

Eventually the subject turned to politics. UGH! He was lecturing me on Hillary Clinton and her basement emails. Like are you telling me how to vote, or would you like to get to know me here?! He sounded surprised when I abruptly started saying goodnight. There are 10 thousand other things I'd rather be doing!

People, have some questions at the ready so that you can have a two-way getting-to-know-you conversation with no major lulls. Pretend you are actually interested in getting to know the person on the other end of the line! If you aren't, it's time to bail! I'm not here for your listening pleasure; I want a partner I can have a conversation with! That means TWO people conversing about something that interests *both* of them. Politics upfront is a no-no. Religion may also be another taboo subject upon first contact. Put the soapbox away until it becomes appropriate.

Snake Charmer

Nice guy; it just didn't pan out. They say there's someone out there for everyone...

My wise friend Beth once said, "If these people had any social skills they wouldn't need to look online. It's easy to hide behind a computer screen." She made a good point, however, I happened to be on there too — and I'm very social. The thinking is, hey I'm a nice, honest, relatively sane person. There must be others out there like me, right? And there are, but they are few and far between. I figure there are worthy choices available if you are willing to search the haystack for the needle. A lot of the same people are online for years, likely because they *are* lacking in social skills (Or, they like having that pool of occasional fresh meat to draw from). It is, however, getting increasingly more difficult to meet people in social settings. House parties aren't as frequent, employers have rules, and if you join an outdoors or other social group you don't want to poop where you eat. Therefore, online dating has become the popular and accepted social norm.

It is so backwards though! Think about it! You see photos you want to believe are accurate, you read words you hope are accurate, and *then* you agree to talk to the person *to discern whether or not* you'd like to meet and see how it goes. That is quite the opposite of approaching someone you are attracted to across a crowded room, and talking to him/her hoping the personality matches the appearance. The process of getting to know the person starts immediately as you begin conversing live, complete with facial expressions and tone. It's a much better system than scanning oh so many ads and praying to the gods that it works out this time!

We do what we must (until we need a break from the process).

Bedlam Bound

I've had policeman friends tell me that security guards and prison guards often equate themselves as brothers in blue, but in truth the cops don't recognize this. My potential date was a (cop wannabe) security guard who sure thought he was above the law. He'd bragged (and you know what I say about braggarts!) about being the captain of security at a local school (such power!), how he had a service dog, blah blah blah. I knew the type and treaded lightly. He had given so much personal info upfront that I was able to find him on FB and saw some photos he no doubt purposely left off his ad. To put it mildly, the online ad photos were far away and blurry in order to (deceive) diminish his bad skin and shorter stature. *No Bueno!*

Besides the fact that I just wasn't attracted to (his arrogance) him, our conversations weren't going well and I had zero interest. He kept texting and I would politely give one-word answers back, which should've been an indication I wasn't interested, but he wasn't having it. The only reason I didn't spell it out clearly for him was *because* I know the type...

Eventually, I stopped responding. That's when the evil texts began. He proceeded to tell me I was no good, would never find a decent man because I'm a total game player, a cruel biotch who rips men's hearts out of their chests... Yup, that's me! The femme fatale out to get him personally! Truth about madness is, when we point out another's faults as he did, we're really talking to a mirror. We point out in other people what we unconsciously believe about ourselves deep down, which is exactly what he was doing with some of the things he'd elucidated (will never find a good person because you're no good, etc.). Also, he'd clearly been let down in the past and was (damaged goods) down on women for not parting the waters for him.

Normally, I'd let that noise go. Not worth engaging in a battle of wits with the likes of him, but I took his cheap bait because I felt he needed a lesson of his own. He needed to hear, as gently as I could muster, that he was sounding insecure, behaving badly and would never find a good woman until he addressed his angry demons. Of course this didn't go over well, and he gave it back to me both barrels. I'd been polite up till that point, but he crossed a line and while I should've let it drop right there, I wasn't about to let him get away with the rotten things he'd said. I'd gotten angry outbursts from insecure men before and wisely let it go easily enough, but this man was asking for it with his scary threats. That was his arrogance, immaturity and insecurity talking. With nothing to lose, I fired back then made it clear he was Bedlam bound and wasn't to contact me again. I ended it with, "Go ahead and have the last word, I'm done here," as I knew he wasn't about to let it end there. Sure enough, he wrote back with more choice names for me, and said he knew I wouldn't allow him the last word so have at it. Ah, no thanks, no more cheap bait will be taken—you, Mr. Scary, are *off the planet!*

Pretty insecure for a *security* guard. From what I'd seen on FB, looks like his cute young wife left him, and surely that didn't do anything for his aging ego. Cleanup in aisle five! What a mess!

I'm not seeking movie star looks; it doesn't matter so much to me as I've grown enough to know we must look on the inside. I've told you I was married to a hot guy and it ended badly. I'm now seeking a man of integrity. I do admit, however, there has to be some mutual attraction for there to be chemistry. This is especially true for men. If they don't have the desire to kiss you on the first date, it ain't happenin'! That was your chance to win them over with personality. Starting as friends is a great place to build a foundation — but it won't be a *strong* foundation if you start off with lies and doubt! You've heard me point out that people *become* handsome to you once you get to know them more. *As time goes on, I realize just what you mean to me... Color my world with hope of loving you.*

Boozin' Belcher

This man has been duly dubbed for the obvious. He seemed to have no problem burping with every sip of his beer. I understand we get comfortable with our mates and, over time, start passing gas in front of each other — be it from above or below. Still, some of us may say something like "Excuse me" afterward. It's called manners. I expect a man to be well-mannered, especially upon first meeting! If not, we're looking at a red flag that potentially screams of low class. "Nice guy, too bad he burps loudly in public. Can't take him anywhere!"

It didn't help that he had five kids at home, which might explain the cray cray... Nothing wrong with kids, I like 'em just fine. Thing is, the age of your kids — or the fact that you never had any — can make or break a relationship. It's all about where you are in life. He was an older man with younger kids, and in need of a sounding board. Not a good situation for most single women. I had no kids at the time myself (he'd neglected to tell me he had custody of so many kids) so this was not what I was looking for.

If you are a man with small children at home, a woman may assume you're looking for a mother for said kids, whether it's true or not. Even if the kids have a mom who is active in their lives, your date is going to need parental skills if she's going to survive a weekend in your home. Likewise, if a woman has five kids, a man may look at this like a burden, especially if his kids are older and independent. Also, it's not always easy to find a babysitter, especially for a larger family. Only a man who loves kids and is looking to be needed will want this situation. They do exist!

I still have a teen at home, so I'm in the zone. I could go either way as she's older and nearly ready to leave the nest. But to say I'd enjoy dating a man with very young children? He's needed by them first, with little time for me, as it should be. Just because his priorities are in the right place, however, doesn't mean I'd be happy with that arrangement — not unless I was allowed to be a part of their lives (eventually meeting and going places together, etc.). I want a person I can do things with, not someone who keeps me on the back burner till he has a free night.

Kids are expensive; whether he's got custody or not, unless he's a deadbeat (RUN!! I have zero respect for a man who won't support his kids!), he's paying out. That doesn't leave much in the budget for dating if he found the time. I can hear you saying, "Dating doesn't have to be expensive!" No, it does not. But it's also not likely to be romantic watching TV with your date when one tyke is begging you to read a book while another is telling you he's hungry, and yet another is hacking up a lung crying for Mommy. Unless you're in the zone... Dating should be fun; where's the fun in that?!

A woman who's never had kids is likely lacking in patience to deal with kids, never mind not knowing how to talk to them, how to entertain them, etc. That's not to say childless women don't love kids and have auntie skills, but being a parent is altogether different. You know how parents can't tolerate that screaming baby in a restaurant, but, "It's different when it's your own"? Yeah, it's like that. I can love a partner's kids as my own, because it would be like they are, but you still have to get to that point. If I have no parental skills, my frustration may outweigh my desire to learn and tolerate. Kids should not just be tolerated; they come with the package. If your partner senses you don't like his/her kids, you can pretty much bet the deal's off! So it makes sense to find someone who has children around the same age(s) as yours. You're basically in the same place in life. Much easier to take two kids around the same age somewhere, rather than trying to please two kids who are too far apart in age to share quality 'family time' interests.

Today, as a mother and teacher, I could've been very helpful to this man and his children. I just don't feel it's my job to teach them the etiquette skills and structure they undoubtedly aren't getting at home. There's only so much I can do with kids who are exposed to a belching crazy mon. It's none of my business anyway. And by his own admission, at the end of the day — after working and then caring for his kids — he's too tired to meet the needs of a partner. If a man like this can get past the dating phase, he just may land a woman who's a perfect fit in his life. Until then, he's going to spend a small fortune in babysitters and cheap beer as he interviews sounding boards.

That Guy

That Guy was hot! I thought I was looking at my next mistake for sure. Didn't take long to realize it was a mistake alright. Yet another meal in exchange for being a sounding board for negativity as he bashes his latest ex. Really didn't need the free meal that badly. Sometimes yer just better off dining alone! (MEET FOR COFFEE!)

If you do find yourself yawning as someone's sound board, *really listen* to what he's saying. We all know That Guy on social media who whines about how he gave his (gorgeous) girlfriend everything under the sun, only to get burnt! And suddenly, *all women are crazy!!* We give him the sympathy he's trying to elicit, even though he's bashing our kind to our face, because we women are compassionate creatures by nature. However, what we *really* want to say is, "Grow a sack, pal! Admit that you made a superficial choice and now you are paying the price the hard way for having thought with the head with the hole in it!! When's the last time you dated anyone who was *not* a perfect 10, you shallow prig! Newsflash — nobody's perfect! If a woman is a total knockout on the outside, *chances are* she's flawed on the inside — *but you didn't look there!* No, you made your depthless choice and now we're all supposed to feel sorry for your stoopid arse!" **#nobodycares**

Saddest part of all? He's going to repeat that pattern. That's who he is! Once he's dusted himself off and gotten (over himself) back on the horse, he will again be seeking out the prettiest woman in the room, only to go off on his heated whiny spiel when his next Barbie kicks him to the curb after using him for everything he's got. Aaaaaand round and round we goooooo!

If you are on a date with a man who is whining about how he got burnt by his (totally hot — and he will tell you this!) former girlfriend, RUN! He is That Guy.

While most men are genetically wired to look for the most attractive female to them, some have managed to control those urges and *look on the inside*. That's the man I'm looking for. Why would I want a superficial man anyway? I'd be starving myself out of fear that if I gained 20 lbs., he'd be kicking me to the curb! You can count on it. He's That Guy. Why would I want to live in fear like that?! It's not healthy for anyone!

Here's the ironic part. That Guy typically has a lady on the side he likes to talk to. She's the fat friend he doesn't want to have sex with. But he tells her his deepest secrets and desires, what's going on in his life, likes having meaningful conversations with her — and she's the first one he goes to for sympathy when Barbie dumps his sorry a$$!

To reiterate: None of us is perfect. If you choose a person based solely on physical attraction and some superficial/sexual chemistry, you can bet your sweet patootie things are going to end miserably. No one can be *that* perfect on the outside without having some imperfections on the inside. Believe it. Get to know someone — someone who has common interests outside the bedroom — before you jump into anything. You may still be fooled in the end, but relationships always come with some amount of risk, eh? It's still worth putting your heart on the line for. Go ahead and take that risk — just be aware of the odds!

Mr. Roboto, Incommunicado

I was performing at a local comedy club and made the mistake of mentioning it to a potential dater. I say this is a mistake because it gives the lurker the upper hand, whereas he can check *me* out, but... He said he might show up. After the show, he texted me via the dating site to say he'd thought I had a great show. Then things got weird...

Lurker: I saw you but you didn't say hi!

Me: Where were you?

Lurker: At the bar! I was wearing a Hawaiian shirt (NOOOOO!) with a blazer, couldn't miss me!

Me: (But I did. Like how was I supposed to know?? Déjà vu, see The Nut) Why didn't you make yourself known?

Lurker: You were talking to your friends. I didn't want to interrupt.

Me: <blink blink> Well then?!? (HELLOOOOOO!)

I don't recall why we never met after that, but I can guess. I have a strong personality, which can be intimidating for some men. If he's (low on testosterone) that shy, we ain't a match! I'm pretty sure he sensed this.

It's not wise to give a stranger the upper hand. Don't tell these people *where* you work until you've ruled out insanity

Random Stuff
&
Strategic Plotting

The Story of the Pencil

The pencil maker took the pencil aside just before putting him into the box. "There are five things you need to know," he told the pencil, "before I send you out into the world. Always remember them and never forget, and you will become the best pencil you can be.

ONE: You are capable of doing great things, but allow yourself to be held in someone's hand for guidance.

TWO: You will experience a painful sharpening from time to time, but that suffering will help you to become a better pencil.

THREE: You will be able to correct any mistakes you might make.

FOUR: The most important part of you will always be what's inside. Pay attention to what's happening there!

AND FIVE: Everything you do will leave a mark, so try to be conscious of that in your every action."

~Adapted from the same title by Paulo Coelho

I'm adding my own number SIX: You can't write the next chapter if you keep rereading the last one, and looking ahead is a waste of time since you don't know what the future holds. Live in the moment, and be open to surprises!!

There Are Rules!!

Recap of nonnegotiable rules for online dating:

1) No giving them your address!
2) Meet in a public place, and always have your own transportation!
3) Trust your instincts! If s/he seems like bad new, s/he prolly is!!
4) The red flags are there! Watch for them, and be ready to RUN!
5) Be selective, you're worth it! But also be open and kind.
6) Carry emergency money!
7) No one can use you without your permission. Use your head (not the one with the hole in it!).
8) There's no shame in seeking help if you need it!!!

Watch out for Negative Nellies/Davey Downers, and people who tell you what they *don't* want. Dating should be fun and romantic, light and airy! If you're feeling like a sounding board ("My wife left me for another man, took everything... My kid is in trouble... I'm in between jobs right now..."), RUN! There's no future in it. S/he's not in a good place, and won't be anytime soon. Unless you're a licensed therapist looking for pro bono work off the clock, s/he's not your problem. Remember my Davey Downer, whom I actually kinda liked, but couldn't stand the dark conversations on dates. It seemed like he needed a friend though, so I knocked him down to the Friend Zone. That just meant I still had to listen to the misery, but now I was paying for my own meals. What was in it for me?! This wasn't good dating, or a good friendship! Taking care of self is a good thing. Make sure your dates are FUN!

Take Notes

I've mentioned how people online often become Houdinis after texting a bit, and for that reason I have a system of cataloguing the men I've connected with on my cell phone. I'll often write the contact name as something like "Joe in Webster, 45, Plenty of Sharks". Sometimes these folks resurface a few months after ghosting, so it helps to have this system at your fingertips.

Why do they disappear, only to return about three months later? My theory is that they always have about five possibilities — people they are talking to besides you. When it appears they are going to get lucky with a certain one they are interested in, they drop you like a hot potato. Then, as mentioned earlier, something happens around the three-month mark. It's an actual thing, if you research it. Called the Honeymoon Phase, this phenomenon seems to end after getting to know each other for three months. At this point, you start to see the person's true colors, the thrill of the newness has died down, and often that's the breakup point if the relationship doesn't have what it takes to last.

When this happens, the seekers go back to their little black book and look you up, losing nothing if you don't take the bait. (Bait is cheap!) At that point, you can decide if the person is worth your time (Not!). I have had several men resurface; I've also gotten butt dialed, late-night drunken calls, etc. But I digress... Keeping the numbers catalogued in this way will help you organize the potential daters in your head. If you're like me, the memory has faded, and these little notes can be very helpful when I get a call!

Sex Talk

It's amazing to me how often I start chatting with a new man and the conversation gets steered toward sex by them. No matter what you do to dissuade it, they try to bring it right back around. Some don't wait long at all! I am prepared for it, since my dad taught me well that this is how men are wired, but there's such a thing as self-control. Have some! Show enough class to wait until we are further along and comfortable with each other before you go and (send me a pic of your junk) steer the conversation into the gutter. They have 900# operators standing by for just $3.99 a minute if that's what you're after! Don't call me for that, call them — you'll get a pro!

If you are doing this to a woman, you are sending a very clear message — that you are interested in only one thing. Not taking the bait; move along! Either clean up your act if it's a classy woman you want, or find a bimbo who'll talk dirty to you. I'm sure eventually you'll strike gold (diggers).

I figure if a guy wants to know more about my favorite sex position than my favorite food (or color, whatever), that's a red flag waving. He's not classy enough to date me. Oh sure, mebbe some women like this, and that's OK — plenty of men have told me that the women are just as bad! They will send nudie pics of themselves and ask for one in return. I've never solicited such a pic from men I've dated awhile, never mind men I haven't even met yet! Still, with all the pics I've received from said men, my next book could easily be a coffee table pop-up book of penises!

It all goes back to putting your best foot forward. If it's temporary love you're looking for, so be it. I sincerely doubt a relationship that begins with sex talk is going to be a love to last through the ages. Be classy in your responses to women. If you are telling a woman straight off the bat that you find her sexy and would like to kiss her all over, it could be a turnoff. At least it would be to me.

If you read the headline to this part and thought I was going to mention talk during sex, better known as pillow talk, I might as well <shrug>. What *is* that?! Do men really think we women find this sexy? It's more of a guy thing, methinks. Mebbe some women like that, but discussion amongst my lady friends would suggest otherwise. Communicate what you like with your partner, by all means, but some of the phrases I've heard were just plain bizarre and a major turnoff! I think because some men wish we'd engage in (nasty) sex talk during the act, they do it thinking we want to hear it! UGH! OK, mebbe if the words were carefully chosen — romantic, lyrical, perhaps in Italian, I could get into it. But no, I want to firmly whisper, "SHhhhhhhh, don't talk!"

I'll go one step further… I read about a man who sued his wife when he learned she'd been faking orgasms throughout their entire marriage. HE WON! My thing is, Why fake anything?! To stroke the fragile male ego? Oh hell no! I want the orgasm too! I'm not letting him off that easy! If a woman is faking orgasm, she wants you off her as soon as possible. I suppose if a couple has been married a very long time, a woman may feel justified in this — She still did her part in giving him the release he sought. But in the process, his male ego was wounded.

This is a huge phenomenon — protecting the male ego! I have a friend who said he was lying with his girlfriend in bed, and she asked him if he was gay! I asked if there was a particular reason she'd asked this — especially at a most inopportune moment —

like he wasn't touching her or something, but he said quite the opposite. She merely asked because she'd heard a rumor. Could she mebbe have taken another moment to bring up this delicate subject? By the age of 20, EVERY woman should know about the fragile male ego! Another girlfriend had told this same friend — while in bed — that she found his naked body to be unattractive. WHERE did he find these women?! Everyone should've had a dad like mine, who'd clued me in to this. It's a thing!

Inflate my ego gently

Tell them Heaven sent me

Oh 'cause I'm so expressive

And I'm so obsessed

~*Elton John, "Ego"*

Some Surprising Statistics

Statistically speaking, if it's December and a man feels the relationship isn't going quite as well as hoped, he will end the relationship around December 9 to avoid having to buy a Christmas gift. At that point, he will stay single through March to also avoid having to spend money on Valentine's Day. With spring fever right around the corner, it's a safe bet March 1 is a good time to post an ad if you're giving this a try.

Then there's the flip side. One year I had SEVEN men crawl out of the woodwork on February 14 to ask if I had plans for Valentine's Day, and one on the 15th to suggest we meet even though I had considered us incompatible a year before. This Hallmark holiday seems to wreak havoc on the lonely. We think of it as a girls' holiday, however, I've come to see that lonely, romantic men take it just as hard as women, perhaps even more so! These men wear their masks of false bravado well, but feel far more than we give them credit for.

It may be said of him that Cupid hath clapped him o' the shoulder but I'll warrant him heart-whole.

~William Shakespeare

You might think the sites that charge a monthly fee are better. I myself reasoned that someone paying money must be seriously looking for someone, as I am, and therefore prepay sites would produce more quality prospects. Imagine my surprise when the opposite held true! I went right back to the freebies. There are lots of people out there not wanting to pay for a dating service, which doesn't necessarily mean they are cheap, unworthy or not seriously looking. I found a lot more men on the free sites were willing to come out and meet me than the ones hiding behind a screen paying money to 'meet' someone.

According to Statistic Brain (http://www.statistic-brain.com/online-dating-statistics/), of the roughly 54 million single people in the US, 49 million have tried online dating. This equates to about $1,749,000,000 of annual revenue for the online dating industry, with the average person spending $243 per year. Ten percent of those users will give up (likely out of frustration with what they've experienced) within the first three months.

Depending on where you live, although the population of single women is slightly greater in the US, 52.4 percent of users are men, with 47.6 percent being women. With men being universally friskier by nature, methinks it makes perfect sense there are slightly more men online looking. Seventy-one percent believe in love at first sight (although they rate shared interests as being a bit more important than looks). Thirty-three percent of women will sleep with a man on the first online dating encounter. Keep in mind that, statistically speaking, in most cases you will never hear from the man again if you sleep with him on the first date — no matter how good you were in the sack or amazing you are otherwise!

My old friend Jeff once told me, "NEVER ever sleep with a guy on the first date! He will go home and think, 'How many other men has she done this with?!' and he won't call the next day!" As mentioned previously, it's apparently OK (and practically expected these days) to bed him on the second or third date. A smart woman will make him wait; a man who is truly interested in you will oblige.

More than once, I've had to tell a man he was moving too fast. Sometimes, when you tell them this, they get really offended! Oh well! NOT your problem! I don't consider this normal. It's not personal; I'm not saying you're not desirable, I'm merely saying I'm not ready to get naked with you so soon. If that bothers you, then you clearly don't respect boundaries. Red flag, Mr. Emo!

I told my friend Heidi of a statistic I'd read claiming that, of all the singles looking, there are far more available good women out there than men. Ever the optimist, she immediately poo-pooed this saying emphatically, "Oh, I don't believe that!" followed by, "That's negative thinking. If that's what you're going to believe then that's what you're going to attract." When considering the power behind the Law of Attraction, you put out there what you want, rather than feeling defeated by not being able to get what you desire based on statistics. Food for thought. Think positively! Allow yourself this gift.

Scams

Con artists of all kinds know that most people looking for love are vulnerable and trusting. They can sniff out this vulnerability through certain things you say, and work their magic getting you to trust them. While you are likely in no physical danger because you will never meet, you must be very careful nonetheless. They can be very dangerous in other ways. Protect your privacy! Anytime someone is trying to get you to share private information, such as your email or home address, remind yourself this person — no matter how trustworthy s/he seems — is still a stranger! RED FLAG WAVING!

Nigerian Love Scams — Originating in Nigeria and typically run by Nigerians pretending to be Italian. This is a scheme in which someone will be in daily contact with you (only for about ten minutes though, so busy with work) in order to quickly gain your trust. They will try to get you off the site so you're focused solely on them, move very fast with loving words/poems, gain your faith and trust, ask for your address so they can send you flowers (which they will, using stolen credit cards). Eventually, they will say they are flying into your area on business and would like to meet. On the agreed upon day, you will get an urgent call saying s/he is stuck at the airport, some immigrations passport problem — and that s/he needs you to wire money right away. Amazingly, many lonely hearts fall for this and it is extremely hard to prosecute since there is no paper trail (See Tony the Tiger).

Here are the tell-tale signs of a Nigerian Love Scammer. They are almost always:

*Widowers

*Have one older school-age child living at home (heart-strings!)

*Living far from you

*Making good money, but overseas — "Must travel a lot for the job!"

*Foreign born, usually Italian (but the accent doesn't match the country)

*Will call you terms of endearment right away like "Baby"

*Will call every night to earn your trust and ask you to close your ad. May try to skype one-way

*Will text romantic poetry, and send flowers if given your home address

Catfishing — These people will try to lure you into a relationship with a fictional online persona — life stories and photos they stole from other online profiles (and there is no way to prevent this) — in order to make you fall in love. More psychological in nature, these con artists want to be someone they're not, and have a life they don't have. Their fake persona can be anything they wish they truly were, giving them lots of friends and attractive qualities they wish they had. It cannot go on forever, though. Eventually, they will slip up, or you will call them to the carpet for not coming out to meet you. If catfishers took truth serum, they would sound something like this: "Just hand me your personal information while I screw with you and your family for $#!ts and giggles!" It's an emotional high for them. If your person is wanting to text forever without meeting (distance will be their excuse), time to $h!t or get off the pot!

Phishing — This is a fraudulent scam where you would receive emails, supposedly from a reputable company, inducing you to reveal personal information, such as passwords and credit card numbers. Online dating sites are a good place for scammers to look for victims because they know what loving things you want to hear. They know once they earn your trust, you might willingly share your personal info with them. Truth be told, many can get your email address right away by claiming they are not a subscriber to the dating service and can only communicate via emails (but then how did they initially get the message to you?!). They will first send you their email address, using secondary servers such as Hotmail or Yahoo. If someone offers an email address asking you to contact them (in which they can then see your address), report it on the dating site!

Identity Theft — These scammers are looking to rob your personal info, especially your credit card information, for financial gain. This can cause an array of expensive legal problems and may tarnish your credit record for a very long time. Identity theft has ruined many a life as it is so hard to undo the damage once done. If you suspect your credit card info has been compromised in any way, report it to the respective bank(s) right away!

Ghosting — Dictionary.com defines ghosting as "The practice of suddenly ending all contact with a person without explanation, especially in a romantic relationship." This is actually very common, for men and women alike. These are the people I've referred to throughout the book as (cowards) Houdinis. Everything seemed to be going along great and then suddenly, *POOF!*. With ghosting there is no ending conversation, perhaps because confrontation would be too difficult or not worth the trouble. Whatever the reason, the act of ghosting effectively ends a relationship, usually before you've even met to establish one.

There's no warning, no apology, no excuse. It's hard not to take it personally, but try not to. You've done nothing to warrant it, and may never know the real reason it was done to you. Don't even bother wasting your time telling them off; they obviously don't care! The 'ghoster' wasted enough of your time. Move on right away, knowing you dodged the bullet of someone who isn't a straight shooter.

Tips for Writing Your Ad

There are actually classes you can take for helping you create a winning ad. "Write a more enticing ad to lure the love of your life! Learn what to say to attract the right mate! Prepare for an amazing first date! No cynical feelings, only positive experiences!..." Gag me! All hokey marketing tools to make money. You can do this yourself! Speak from the heart, watch out for double entendres, and write an ad that will attract a specific reader — the person you want! Know your intended audience. If, for example, you want an educated person, throw in a few big words to show that you are pretty smart yourself! It may not dissuade the undesirables, but will surely draw the intellectuals!

I want to spend the last third of my life laughing (not a lot to ask). For that, I need a man with an amazing sense of humor. Someone who gets me, and vice versa. Thing is, it seems everyone online has a self-proclaimed "great SoS". Don't *tell me* you're witty and intelligent, *show me* throughout your ad!

Include the qualities you want in a mate (people appreciate this), however, instead of listing your own, depict yourself as having those qualities and follow it with something like, "Seeking someone with similar qualities" or "Seeking like-minded person".

Everyone wants someone who's honest, loyal, has a sense of humor, blah blah blah. Avoid being cliché! We all love holding hands during moonlit walks on the beach… Shine by making your ad stand out! Read what other people have to say in their ads, then be creatively different with yours!

Men like to hear adjectives like kind, loyal, caring and passionate. If you are Plain Jane, keep it simple — I like cooking, gardening and affection. This will surely attract the Average Joes who don't want to read verbose ads or draw what they perceive to be a high-maintenance woman. If, however, you are seeking something more, tell us who you are and exactly what you're looking for in a man! You'll get far fewer responses but higher quality ones, and be more likely to snag the fish you want.

Women like to hear words like dependable, one-woman man, faithful in all ways. Women also love funny men, so go ahead and let your personality show through, rather than telling us how freakin' funny you are! If you're a biker chick, don't say you love a man who rides a motorcycle, as this will dissuade the nice guys who wish they could afford one. Instead, word it in such a way that you are "biker friendly" or "motorcyclists welcome".

Lastly, and perhaps most importantly, be honest and up-front! You can be anyone you want in writing, but what happens when it comes time to actually meet?! $#!T just got real! Don't tell us what baggage you have. Do use current photos, describe your body type accurately, and know what you want. If you have a sexual fetish, find a way to *discreetly* put it in there. A vague ad may get you quantity but not quality. A *very* vague, effortless ad may get you zero responses.

Conversely, you may want to avoid being too verbose. Most men are admittedly lazy — they don't want to have to read too much! Then again, I've heard it said that more intelligent men appreciate more detail, so if that's who you want to attract... Remember, you don't want crumbs, you want the whole cookie! Put the effort in!

Tips on Photo Posting

Lack of a photo is a red flag! Why is s/he hiding? Is s/he married? Fugly? Most likely, anyone you (try to) chat with who hasn't posted a photo is going to ignore you or ghost on you. Someone who is sincerely looking for a partner knows how important it is to post a photo. If I have to, why don't you? Fair is fair! If your ad doesn't include a photo, most people won't even look at it! The only people who would answer a personal ad that doesn't have a photo are people who know they can't be choosey — usually others who don't want to post their pic either! Things that make ya go Hhhhhmmm…

Posting no more than three really good photos is best. You only want three great pics because — and you've prolly done this yourself — when people are skimming through your photos they will dismiss you at the first one they see that they don't like! Ask a friend or two (especially friends of the opposite sex!) to look at the pics to make sure they are all attractive, complimentary and look like you, yet without being too showy. Your job is to sell yourself, not pimp yourself!

Photos should be accurate and current, as you will eventually be called out when it's time to meet someone. Why start off with a lie? Also, avoid photos you are not in! Nobody is impressed with landscape pics, your house, cute memes, etc. I'm not looking to date your boat or your dog; post a pic of you with your dog, and now I'm interested!

Do not post pics of yourself with a former significant other, or any attractive member of the opposite sex unless that person is your relative — and it says as much in big letters in the photo description! And when you post a pic of yourself with others, make sure it's clear which one is you! If I'm prolly gonna find your friend a lot more attractive, ya might wanna blacken his face, you know, for his privacy.

Gentlemen — really, not many women are going to be impressed with your shirtless bathroom selfie (toilet in the background, sheesh!), or you holding a big fish. Spending the day drinking beers on your buddy's boat does not make you a masculine gatherer/hunter. It's a fish on a string. Not sexy.

We are also not big fans of the car selfie, where your KGB shades are blocking your pretty eyes. Women look at eyes first! Who's behind those Foster Grants? We don't know, we can't see you! I get it, you think you look badass, and women do love the bad boys, but you're prolly wearing a cap too. And a baseball cap screams I'M BALD! Guys, we assume most men have lost hair by middle age. Gonna wear it to bed, too? Your cap isn't showing us who you really are, it just hides what YOU perceive to be a flaw. Show us that beautiful chrome dome you own! No surprises! Trust that most women are forgiving, accepting creatures. We hope that you will do likewise, overlooking our muffin top. Fair is fair.

Ladies — the guys want at least one full-body shot in there, as they are visual creatures and want to see the whole package before deciding if you're worthy. Do post an attractive pic, but do not have too much cleavage showing. Forget the bikini pic no matter how tempting it is. He'll likely ask you for more pics once you make contact anyway, so save it for then IF you choose to share. You want sexy and classy, not trashy. If you post trash, you will attract trash.

I sometimes appear smaller in photos than in real life. When it comes time to meet someone I suspect may be shallow, I feel the need to put it out there that I'm Rubenesque. As soon as I say "Objects may be larger than they appear," you know he's running for the hills. Anyone can look good thanks to a creatively cropped photo (Hey, we are here to sell ourselves, right? Ad is short for advertisement!). It's important to be upfront so there are no surprises when you meet. If you walk with a cane, if you wear glasses sometimes, whatever s/he needs to know in order to find you in the café — disclose the fact. Even if there is chemistry, even if you are very attractive otherwise, s/he will be fixated on 'the lie' and can't get past it. Save the skeletons for another time, though! We're talking appearance only here!

To reiterate — If the picture doesn't match the actual person when you meet, that's a deal breaker for most people. You can laugh and joke for hours, but in the end it just ain't gonna happen. Most men want an instant attraction*, whereas women are much more tolerant of looks, getting to know the person and letting the chemistry build. But we are still cognizant of the fact that you *lied*. You're a beautiful person! At the risk of being redundant… Ever notice when you give someone a chance, s/he becomes good looking to you, even though you wouldn't have given that person a second look passing on the sidewalk before now? But I digress. Use good, current photos, people! You are selling yourself, so yes, be sure to use flattering pics, but never misrepresent! It's unforgivable to some.

*Since men are visual creatures seeking instant attraction, they want that trophy on their arm. While the thin beauties are by far the most sought after, there are some men out there who do prefer a Rubenesque figure. They take the time to get to know the person inside and suddenly find her beautiful.

It's a shame that people can be deceitful and ruin it for the others. More often than not, once you graduate to texting, a man will say, "Send me a picture!" Yes, men are very visual creatures;

I get that. Women think very differently from men. All I am hearing in that moment is, "I will judge your worthiness based on the pic you send me in the next five minutes." Pressure is on! Mebbe he wants to know your photos aren't 15 years old because he's been lured in like that before. At that point, I consider that he may be shallow. Whatever happened to "It's what's on the inside that counts"? No, I will not send you a photo. If you can't tell from the three pics I have already posted in my ad, if you don't want to meet me based on the great phone conversations we've had — I'm all set! NEXT!

And don't send me a picture of your junk! What IS IT with men doing this, totally unsolicited?! If two consenting adults agree to exchanging nudies, fine, but why would you take that lack of privacy risk? Is this putting your best foot forward? Not if you're looking to meet a quality person it's not!

Because women are far more tolerant of men's flaws, the men can get away with finding the trophy wife — even if they ain't all that. To these men I want to say, "Dood! Have you seen a mirror lately?! You may think you're still the football hero, but hellooo, that was 40 years ago!! WHY are you posting your high school photo when you look nothing like that now?!" Hey, it's human nature, and my little lecture won't change the world. It is what it is. Men are the hunters, and are selective in the hunt. My thinking is to sit back to wait for the lions to find me, as I know from experience that if I write to a guy, most likely (unless he's really shy or really needy), he's not going to write back. Just a simple fact in my experience — most men don't like aggressive women (unless she's a Barbie). Go ahead and be proactive if that's your personality! Nothing wrong with going after what you want. I just figure anyone who likes my photos will write to me, and then I know I'm talking to someone who's attracted to me — and we're halfway there!

One of the popular free dating sites has a Meet Me feature where you can choose people you'd like to meet, based solely on their primary photo. It involves simply clicking Yes or No (an X or a check mark), and you're immediately brought to the next person's photo, all of whom are persons supposedly selected just for you per your search criteria. You know what I hear in my head every time I get a PING! on my phone that "SOMEONE WANTS TO MEET YOU!"? I visualize a man, any random man, sitting with his phone and swiping: "I'd do her (swipe right)... Not her (swipe left)... I'd do her twice (swipe right)... her... She'll do in a pinch... OK... no way her... absotively not her... Meh... DAMN! ... Her... Aw, hell no!" It's a superficial feature that gets you nowhere. If you are also attracted to the people who've selected you (and there's a Mutual Attraction alert to help you out with that), you need only upgrade to a paying account to contact them. But chances are, if you were to diligently scroll through all the photos till you found him/her, and wrote a message, s/he would not respond. You were just an impulse swipe during a lunch break. If they are truly interested, they will contact you.

Making even one minor change to your ad bumps it up to the forefront, as though it's a new ad, but the regular subscribers will still recognize your main photo. If your ad isn't getting responses, change the main photo — swap it out from one of the others you have or post an updated one — and see what happens!

Tips for Reading Into an Ad

People often tell us things without actually saying it or even realizing it! When a man says he's a hard worker, that's supposed to be a good thing, right? Not always in this case. Hey, it's great to be a hard worker, and proud of it! However, in my extensive experience <ahem>, I've discovered that some men put this out there because they're compensating for something. In my mind I'm hearing, "My wife left me! ME!, who worked SO hard to provide for her, and she didn't appreciate it! No, she went out and found herself (a better lover) another man (because I was never around)!" I'd be more impressed with words like "strong work ethic" or "love my job but have time for you". These phrases indicate character rather than bitterness.

I feel horrible saying this, but it's the truth — This screams I am Average Joe! Hey, there's absotively nothing wrong with Average Joe, at all. He's likely a sweet and loving, dependable guy! As mentioned, I just feel he's best paired with Plain Jane, which is who this term will likely draw. He should give her a chance! Why go after an exciting woman when you can see the writing on the wall — you will never be able to keep her satisfied! Average Joe can live a very comfortable life with Plain Jane. Lots of women tire of all the dating games as we mature, and are more likely to settle down with Average Joe for stability. But remember — there's a difference between being content, and being happy. As long as you're settling down in life and not settling down on a mate, it's all good.

Psychologically speaking, people who are adamant about who they are (or aren't) are usually hiding something. For instance, if a person must specify "I DO NOT LIE!" then you can bet your next paycheck s/he's a liar. You can also assume he's been lied to, and didn't appreciate it one bit (damaged goods). I prefer phrases like "old-fashioned values" or "high moral standard" to angry aggression.

Got a message from someone who lives super far away? Chances are, s/he is just looking for a text buddy. Perhaps the person is married. Either way, they KNOW you're not going to hop on a plane or drive eight hours for a cup of coffee, turn around and head back if/when it doesn't work out. People like to have someone checking in on them every day. There's a high you get when someone sends you a spontaneous text, makes you laugh, makes your day. We enjoy, even crave the attention. This may also coincide with the "Don't $h!t where you eat" rule though, whereby people contact others who live far away so they can hook up once and likely never bump into each other at the local market.

Of course it's possible to overcome distance, fall in love and do the move. It happens! If you are open to this, then fine — you are a patient person. However, if your bells and whistles are sounding, trust the noise! Your gut instincts are seldom wrong! There are married folks who would enter into an emotional affair if things are stale in their marriage. They think there's no harm done since you'll never meet, and you're getting the attention you also crave, but your feelings are in the mix. Unfair!

Some ads are telling even if they don't say much. One man's ad read very simply, something like: "I'm a normal, caring person who works hard. I do like a woman with a large chest." Where to begin… First of all, I could say it shows no class that he mentioned he's a boob man like that. But you know what? I respect what he did there, dissuading the smaller-chested women who don't have a chance. It's honest, something you don't often get online. He knows what he wants and he put it out there. Mebbe if he'd embellished his ad a bit, told me more about himself beyond hard worker and 'I like boobies', I might've been intrigued.

Then there's this. If he signs off "Peace!" you'll want to run! This is almost always indicative of anger issues. Imagine! Sad but true. It's just one of those things you pick up on after having done this for a while. Remember, humans are generally inauthentic to begin with, and when selling themselves the creative marketing begins.

Some other Alison translations at a glance:

A stated height of 5'8" = 5'5" (basically, if he's under 5'8" for real, take off one to three inches)
In-between jobs = can't hold a job
Separated = married! Separated people (or married liars) have unfinished business and have no business starting anything with you! Move along, nothing to see here!
Ball cap = bald cap
Blonde = bald. Or, if he's over 50 and has hair, he's prolly dying it yellow
Drinks moderately = lush
Drinks socially = prolly a lush
Let's meet for drinks = lush
Smokes occasionally = pothead
Loyal = the ex cheated
Hates liars = the ex cheated and lied
Honest = liar
Secure = looking for a younger babe
Financially secure = wanna be yer sugar daddy
Emotionally secure = bat$h!t crazy!
Sane = bat$h!t crazy!
A few extra pounds = obese

Large frame = morbidly obese
Big boned = see Large frame
Big heart = been used
Simple man = boring
Easy going = If he's honest, a sucker. If he's a liar, anger issues
Drama free = drama queen
Low maintenance = boring or judgmental
Normal = boring
Affectionate = horny
Romantic = cries at the drop of a hat
Catholic = nonreligious
Religious = recovering alcoholic
Take care of myself = looking for thin woman
Looking for a relationship = could go either way
Looking for dating/friends only = looking for sex only
No sexpectations = hope to get laid

When People Don't Reply to Your Ad

I'm a polite person and do believe in writing back when someone has taken the time to write to me. For the times I have not written back, it was because either I was overwhelmed with my new ad — up to 30 hits in the first two days — or else the guy had nothing more to say than "Hi". If he can't invest the time and energy to say something more than "Hi", I'm not going to waste my time responding! Why should I, when he only invested a half a second to hook me in?! You can paste "Hi" into 50 ads in record time, hoping SOMEONE will take the bait. It shows zero lack of effort — no matter what they tell themselves to the contrary.

For those who did put forth the energy, but I just wasn't feeling it, I would write back something to the effect of, "Thank you for contacting me. I don't feel we're a match, but wanted to wish you luck in your search!" This lets them down gently without the bad feelings. Sometimes they would write back saying, "Thanks, good luck to you as well." More often than not, though, they would not write back since my message didn't require a response. We both said our piece and moved on. Never has anyone written back to give me a hard time about it (other than mebbe Pennywise, if you include the phone call where he requested a breakdown of why he wasn't The One).

Actually, one man did write back to inquire why I hadn't responded, as it's only polite, and I explained it was because he didn't invest the time and effort to write anything substantial. A simple "Hi" is just lazy! It tells me you are hoping to snag one desperada in the minimum amount of exertion. I suppose that's better than copying and pasting a larger, generic missive, which is usually so transparent and has the same effect — we know you didn't put forth an ounce of energy. He said most women don't write back anyway, so why waste his time? Good point, however, his reasoning is skewed. I understand why he thinks that but if he doesn't make any effort, he won't catch the attention of a quality person. No one wants to feel like s/he is just part of a mass distribution of emails to find someone to talk to. Invest the time in someone you are interested in! Quality over quantity.

For most people online, if they aren't interested they aren't going to respond. Period. Call it tactless, lazy, rude, whatever. They just didn't care enough to bother.

When Your Friend Is on the Same Site

Since most ads run for about three months at a minimum, and area-based, you are likely to come across the same prospects as your friend who is also looking. By all means — compare notes! Just remember that, when comparing potential dates with your friends, we are all different, and possibly looking for different things in a person.

If you dated someone whom you found arrogant, for example, you may find that your friend actually *likes* a person who is a bit arrogant! It can be considered sexy and assertive to some — a turn-on. Just because you had a hard time with it doesn't mean your friend would. To each his own. Explain why you didn't hit it off with that person yourself — why you found the reason to be a red flag — then step aside. Allow your friend to decide if s/he still wants to pursue a meeting with that person anyway. You may think you're doing a valiant thing, sparing your friend from grief, but you may also be standing in the way of true love!

On the flip side, it may happen that you both are attracted to the same person. What then? The Woman's Code suggests you cannot step on your friend's toes if she saw him first. Fair is fair. But suppose the man doesn't want your friend? She has no claim on him, so why should you and he suffer out of some weird sense of honor? Be honest with yourself. If a guy isn't that into you, but

252

is into your friend, step aside and wish them well. They may just go behind your back anyway, and that feels worse! Be adults about it. If it's meant to be…

When Crossing the Line of Friendship

There have been many guy friends over the years with whom I would have loved to have dated, but they just weren't feeling that certain je ne sais quoi. Translation: they didn't want to schtoop me, not even a little. (They'll be sorry when I hit the lottery!) As mentioned previously, any guy who is attracted to you will go through Hell and high water to be with you. And if he gives it the 'ol "Why ruin a good friendship?" you can bet your next paycheck he's lying! When it comes to free sex, most men are a special kinda stoopid, thinking with the head with the hole in it. Yes, they WILL risk a great friendship for that!

It irks me to no end to think the bleached-blonde bipolar Barbie biotches are getting wined and dined by these great guys, but who do the men come running to when they need a sounding board, a gentle shoulder to cry on? The fun fat friend! They complain about how good they were to these women, just don't understand why it didn't work out, blah blah blah. It's *me* they are joking with, *me* they are going to dinners with as I pay for myself, *me* who they confide in. Me who gets tossed aside temporarily when they meet someone new, right there to rekindle the friendship just as soon as their new love crashes and burns. Remind me what I'm getting out of this? Ladies, if he is not initiating contact with you for anything other than your sounding board services, that's an action speaking louder than words. Ask yourself, Is it always me making the first move? If you backed off and let him miss you, what would the result be? If he is truly your friend, he would put forth some effort into said friendship. Are you just a convenience until he finds his next Barbie? If the writing is on the wall — he's neither a true friend, nor ever going to be your boyfriend — move on!

You want him to care but he doesn't. Why waste time pining over someone who clearly isn't interested?! You can tell yourself there are little signs indicating he might change his mind, but these are lies we tell ourselves because we want what we want, and rejection sucks. Stop wasting precious time on someone who doesn't give you the attention you deserve! Clear that out so you can make space for the person who *does* want to spend time with you!

Good communication is key. *You are not only responsible for what you say but for what the other person hears.* To have effective communication, you must be clear! If you want to know something, ASK! Why waste time and energy making frustrating assumptions?! I did this for years until I realized the benefit of clarity. Don't try to read between the lines, ask the questions you really want the answer to. If a person truly isn't interested, s/he will disappear after you call him/her to the carpet. And that's fine. You didn't waste time on someone who wasn't into you. NEXT!

One such male friend engaged in humorous banter with me several times a week. The texting was hilarious, and initially lasted all day long since he was out of work temporarily. Comedy God Robin Williams was born on his birthday and died on mine! Kismet, right?! Eventually, I suggested we take all this fun beyond the cell phones since (texting isn't real!) we shared more than just the same sense of humor — a love of hiking, live music, dining out (who likes to cook for one?), board games, etc. He wholeheartedly agreed. However, when that didn't happen, I confronted him. I pointed out he neither accepted my invitations nor extended his own. Change of heart? In response, I got the anticipated "I've been busy" excuse. By then he had returned to work, so that was valid. However, he then added, "Any free time I have I spend with my (single female) neighbor — some dinners and whatnot, just based on availability." Hhhhhmmm...

I asked if they were dating and he said No, then immediately deflected to how his ex-wife assumed the same after he'd gone fishing with this neighbor and their respective sons. Thing is, I'm very available — with lots of free time (teacher's schedule). Also, I have a car — and I'm not afraid to use it! I could drive to him, casserole in hand, when he can't get free for long. So, what gives?? Calling BS on this one. All I was hearing was that he had time for her, but not me. (If a man wants to be with you...) Whether he was attracted to her or not, she had the upper hand on his friendship, having met his kids, dined in each other's house, etc.

Clearly, he sensed I was interested and did not want to lead me on. OK, but say that! Those little white lies meant to protect my feelings might've worked when I was younger, but I'm an adult now. Let ME handle my emotions when you hit me with the truth! I don't protect my friends with lies. Also, true friends stick around after you call them to the carpet. You're not interested, I get it, but suddenly we can no longer be friends?! Even if a man starts dating someone new, there's no rule he has to throw his female friends aside (and, according to him, he wasn't dating. At least not his neighbor).

> *I want you to want me!*
> *I need you to need me!*
> *I'd love you to love me!*
> *I'm beggin' you to beg me...*
> *(Cue the really cool guitar riff)*

In the week that followed, it was only me initiating contact. We were texting far less frequently — the known risk — and that's fine (Mebbe I'm waaaay off the mark and he's just super busy these days. Mebbe he's lying in a coma somewhere). I'd anticipated this, as it's happened before where a male friend disappeared after I'd hinted at my interest in exploring something more. It's what they do. We didn't stop being 'friends' necessarily — I'm sure I could call either one of these men today and say Hi (but I stubbornly won't) and they'd be receptive. We've just become less significant to each other's life. Lesson learned though. If I were *really* listening, I would've heard the former saying, not in these words, that he just wasn't (attracted) interested.

I polled a few guy pals to figure out why a man would throw away a friendship after a woman suggests it could become more. You're not interested? OK, thanks for your honesty, let's carry on status quo! But no — *POOF*! My analytical mind needs to know why! Cowardice, likely, but I wanted to hear it from a man. The answer I got was a resounding "FEAR!" Apparently, women have great power to put fear into men. Phrases like 'We need to talk' send a guy running to the man cave. I wasn't satisfied with a simple answer that left me with more questions. Fear of what, exactly? That it might ruin a friendship? They'd do that for sex without blinking! That it might work out? Isn't that a good thing!? (Fear of losing a house, I'm told) No, the only answer that made sense to me was that the friendship has now taken a turn in the guy's mind, because he feels you'll be jealous of any woman he then starts dating (But isn't this where he pulls away once things take off with her anyway?). The reason I think this holds water here is because I did call my friend to the carpet by being direct and asking if he was dating his neighbor — the one sentence that likely sent him reeling into the fear abyss.

Bottom line, if my friendship meant enough to him, we might still be in contact. He already has her friendship, and apparently only time enough for one of us. Of course this is all speculation. I wasn't going to hound him for clarity as it wouldn't change the bottom line. Also, getting an honest answer in these situations is like pulling teeth.

It always is harder to be left behind than to be the one to go...
                                                    ~Brock Thoene

When we first met, he'd said his nagging ex-wife was a teacher and now he could never date a teacher again. Huh? (Hhhhhmmm, sound familiar? Refer back to Not For Teacher). I instantly took offense and asked if his ex teaches the lower grades, to which he answered Yes. It does make a difference. Kindergartners and first graders enter school not knowing the expectations of being a student, so those teachers are barking orders all day long, and this can sometimes carry over into their personal lives. It's very different on the secondary level. We do correct behavior all day at high school, but it's less rigid — and I can't imagine I'd need or want to correct my partner's behavior! (Also, I don't bring my work home with me. If I've had a bad day, I will sit in the car outside my home until I've completely detoxed! None of that negative noise in my sanctuary!) His response to this was, "Huh. I'll keep that in mind." What he was likely saying was that he'll consider giving other teachers a chance in the future, but I conveniently read between the lines that he would now consider dating me in the future when he's ready to date again, being newly divorced and all. He was trying to tell me something else. Shame on me for neglecting to ask for clarity in the moment, but his actions told me everything I needed to know.

I was my own worst pabitel (look it up!). These days I'm far choosier who gets to enjoy my time and entertainment. I want to be with friends who want to be with me. Don't waste your time on someone showing the signs you wish were spoken. Ask for clarity right away! "Are you interested in getting together? Yes? Great, when are you available?" Nail that down! If you feel the person is lying, call him/her out on it! If s/he can't commit, there's your answer, but do push for full clarity. Also, if a person won't engage in the tough conversations, that's a red flag. You can bet the runner is a lousy communicator, which is not a good thing in a partner. You can do better!

Repeat after me: Texting. Is not. Real. It's just what lonely people do for attention and/or entertainment until something special comes along. You're special! Of course if you're doing the same thing, then it works — temporarily. But it can end in heartache if you get your hopes up for something more!

> *Tears are words that need to be written.*
> *~Paulo Coelho*

While actions sometimes speak louder than words, we don't really know what the other person is thinking. I made assumptions and misinterpreted. I'd conveniently read between the lines, creating an opening for myself that was never there. He was 'telling' me he wasn't interested, I just didn't (want to) hear it. Instead of asking him flat out if he would like to date me, I wasted precious time reading into his words, analyzing every possibility for an opening. He'd told me about a woman he was interested in and had taken his time getting to know slowly. When they'd gone a couple of days without contact for no particular reason (men have their own schedule, also sometimes test for clinginess in this way) she sent a nastygram to the effect of, "Oh, I *knew* this would happen! It happens all the time!" Her cray cray colors had shone. And that, as they say, was that. But I took this to mean he was letting me know he was getting to know *me* slowly! All I had to do was be patient! And sane!

259

When it still looked like things weren't progressing down the line, I asked for clarity — and got an answer I knew was BS. He wasn't being cruel, just didn't want to hurt me. But guess what? He disappeared soon after, as predicted (an occasional message every now and then, but nothing like it was). This hurt, I won't lie, but it was necessary. You can't make room for the new if you don't clear out the old. Or, as my friend Heidi says, "If you fill up on the appetizer, you won't have room for the main course!" I wanted the appetizer to be my meal, but now I've got the capacity to savor the real meal when it arrives.

> *You.*
> *Not wanting me.*
> *Was the beginning of me wanting myself.*
> *Thank you*
>
> *~Nayyirah Waheed*

Just because he was what I wanted, just because I'd decided I'm a great catch for him, doesn't mean I'm what he wants. And if he's not (attracted) into me, he's not my intended, and prolly not all I cracked him up to be in my psyche. My friend Todd says, "With seven billion people on the planet, I DOUBT there's just "The One" you're compatible with!" True dat.

> *Never allow someone to be your priority*
> *while allowing yourself to be their option.*
> *~Mark Twain*

I thought if I grew the friendship, we'd naturally evolve into more (It does happen — statistically often! Friends sometimes marry down the line, after they've realized 'Nobody knows/loves me better!'). When you can't control it, ya gotta let it go. Since he showed zero interest in spending time with me and nurturing the friendship, I survived by adopting the mantra,

'Your loss, pal! You could've had this! I ain't hangin' around with hope for you anymore. You can't use me for free entertainment when it's convenient for you — not without my permission — I'm nobody's convenience! I'm going to find somebody who *wants* to be with me!'

If you wanna fly,
You got to give up the $h!t
that weighs you down.
~*Toni Morrison*

I still believe that a woman can stay strong with a growing friendship and eventually the man will come to love her, but overall men must be attracted before they'll even give you the time of day. Once you're in the dreaded Friend Zone, it can be difficult to move beyond it! Rare, but it can happen. When the timing is right, you can cross that line and be in love! Just don't hang around waiting for it to happen! Again — live in the moment, enjoy yourself and be open for surprises!

Sometimes life has a cruel sense of humor,
giving you the thing you always wanted at the worst time possible.
~*Lisa Kleypas*

When I told Heidi I missed the laughter, the weekly check-ins, the male energy, the hope of something more down the line, she reminded me I was "settling for crumbs. You want the whole cookie!" Does he ever think of me? Prolly not, but you can't reach what's in front of you until you let go of what's behind you. I do miss our witty banter, and I feel badly that our budding friendship never got to fully blossom, but he has spoken loud and clear and moved on, as I've had to. Reason, Season,

Lifetime. He was a season, and left footprints on my heart. Whether or not he reads this, I thank him for the lesson and hope he's happy in love — the spirit with which this was written.

> *In the end only three things matter:*
> *How much you loved,*
> *how gently you lived,*
> *and how gracefully you let go*
> *of things not meant for you.*
>
> ~*The Buddah*

When Your Date Has Friends of the Opposite Sex

If you are starting a new relationship, you should not have to give up your friends of the opposite sex. These friends have been by your side for years, and deserve better than that. If your new partner asks you to do so, it is a sign of insecurity. Nobody wants a jealous lover. With a secure woman, no problem — she would never expect you to drop a friendship you've been cultivating for years before she arrived. However, an insecure woman might not be as OK with it as you might think. Nobody wants to be thought of as the jealous type though — it's unattractive and reeks of insecurity. Therefore, she may say she is fine with you having female friends but in her private time she is off Googling said woman, stalking her FB page, asking around about her... Believe it! When in doubt, play it safe. Early on in a relationship is not the time to ask your new partner if she wouldn't mind you hanging around with another woman. She knows it's a lot easier to steal something that's not bolted down.

What if she does say it would bother her for you to go out with your gal pal? How would that make you feel? Would you now think less of your new lady? Or would you shrug it off and oblige — as though your old friend didn't matter?! It's got to eat at you on some level! I've known plenty of old-fashioned guys who just wouldn't see their old gal pals out of respect for their new lady, period! I get it, and it's chivalrous, I guess. But we're not kids here. Our mature relationships should reflect our current maturity level.

Unless there's something your partner really wants to do, for example see a certain movie, then it's a really bad idea to leave him/her at home while you see that movie with your gal pal. Why not include both at the movie?! Give them the opportunity to get to know one another in a non-threatening setting. If this old friend is special to you, it just makes sense as they are likely to start seeing more of each other anyway. This takes the sting out of the bite, and allows your new partner to see there is no threat.

If you truly trust your partner, there is no problem. You've each got interests of your own and enjoy some time apart. You usually call on your friends to enjoy these hobbies with. Therefore, your pre-established relationships are a *good* thing. Asking your partner to drop them is so very wrong. If a person asks you to do this, run! DANGER, Will Robinson, DANGER! Red flag waving!

I've been on the receiving end of the dump far too often from male friends who felt they could not see me in order to protect their new lady's feelings. Those relationships never ended well for them. I would get a phone call months or sometimes years down the line, my guy pals wanting back into my life in their loneliness. After I listened to their story of heartache, they would promise never to let this happen again. But guess what? Yeah. Make the decision early on, but anyone who would ask you to drop good friends for their sake is not a healthy person. And if you are dismissing said friendships because of an assumption your girlfriend *might* feel insecure about it, you're not only not communicating effectively, you're not taking care of self or being fair to your old friend. I'll take it a step further too — if a man doesn't accept my gay friends, that's a deal breaker! I'm not giving up any of my friends for anyone, not without just cause.

Some men do something called, for lack of a clinical term, cock blocking. They all know it's done but they don't share that fact with women. It's a way of making sure their guy friends don't sleep with a woman they want to sleep with, or have slept with — even if they never want to be with her again. They are marking their territory. Women do a similar thing, it's just a different C word... We women do this territorial thing when we perceive other women that our guys look at, talk to, or have already been with, to be a threat. Even if the man is not attracted to that other woman, it matters not. If we perceive her to be a threat, she is a threat. We are animals after all.

So, for example, if your partner asks you if you have a problem with him/her seeing a movie with a pal of the opposite sex, you have a dilemma. If you are insecure, things could go either way. Some people have no problem telling you straight out what they think ("OH HELL NO!"). On the flip side, some might say, "Sure, no problem, enjoy yourselves!" When mebbe what they really want to say is, "Are you effing kidding me?? Don't you think I like movies too?! Do you really think you should be hanging out with another man/woman when you are seeing me??!" But that would raise a major red flag in his/her mind that you are jealous and insane. Nobody wants to look insecure, especially before the three-month mark, so we will likely give the answer they want to hear. Then go into stalking mode.

Not all women are insecure. They will encourage you to hang with your female buds and be happy to have some free time for hobbies. I'm just saying insecurity is a real thing for some, and men are generally oblivious to this fact. I've tried to explain it to more than one male friend who thinks I'm absolutely full of it. Gentlemen, the struggle is real. Because men typically think of sex more than women, it's far more likely he'd stray than she would. And she knows you'd ruin a friendship for the free sex if your moral code is skewed. Unless she is very secure and trusting despite being new to you, her radar is on high alert — especially if your friend is a former lover.

A man is going to check out other women; that's a given. Classier men have mastered the subtle art of peripheral vision eye-balling, and he'd never tell his woman he's doing this. He doesn't want to (argue) make her feel insecure, but it's hard to fight that basic human nature. To let my (ex)husband know I was OK with him appreciating beauty, I would point out women for him to check out! "Wow, look at the legs on her!" In this way, he felt OK with looking briefly and I didn't feel threatened at all. I know when to give my man enough rope to hang himself. Keeping him on a short leash is tiring work. No harm in just looking. Peruse the buffet all you like — just so long as you eat at home!

The same goes for men who feel threatened by a woman hanging out with male friends. Unless her friend is gay, the male friend may be a (perceived) threat. Here's the rub. It's healthy to have friends of the opposite sex to bounce ideas off of. You may storm off after an argument, go sit with your old friend and spout, and get his/her perspective on the matter. That can only help improve your relationship with your partner! I still bounce questions off my male friends to better understand the male mind, and enjoy helping them understand the female perspective!

See how unhealthy it sounds to *not* allow your mate some friends of the opposite sex? Why deprive someone of the friendships they've established years prior? It's not fair. Meet these friends with an open mind, and be glad your partner has healthy relationships in his/her life. Chances are, you've finally found an emotionally secure person capable of having a healthy relationship with you!

Remember the dreaded three-month mark? By this time you should know if your relationship is a keeper or not. If it's a strong one, you've already met the other person's friends and formed your opinions. If your friends approve of your partnership (not just the person, but your compatibility with said person), you're golden!

266

The friends With Benefits Arrangement

There's nothing wrong with having an arrangement where, if both parties are in agreement, you share physical intimacy with a friend until one or both of you decides it's no longer serving you. In fact, this seems to be a growing trend as society changes, the traditional family values break down, we get older and lonely… We like the ease of not having to work at a relationship, coming and going as we please, so to speak. An FWB arrangement can offer folks the ability to share intimacy when desired without the "hassle" of commitment. Of course if you have religious or other reasons why you would never consider such an arrangement, then clearly this isn't for you. (Skip to the next section — unless your curiosity is getting the best of you!)

We women are very emotional beings who tend to get attached to a man we (get naked with) make love to, so casual sex without commitment may be hard for some to accept. I admit I had a hard time accepting the "immoral" aspect of such a verbal contract until much later in life. I used to think of FWB as "I don't want to keep you, but I'll do you until something better comes along," but that's a negative belief. What if, instead, you think of it like this: We are two nice people, we just aren't the person we

267

see ourselves growing old with. Let's just enjoy each other's company, sharing intimacy for an indefinite amount of time, living in the moment. We don't have to be alone and depraved right now. We are friends, and hopefully that will never change, but if you can't be with the one you love, ...

Attitude is paramount. As mentioned, I initially struggled with the whole "I'll do you till something better comes along" school of thought. However, dear friends helped me to see that having your physical needs met is not selfish; we are consenting adults, have physical needs as humans, and it's a new millennium where women are freer than ever before to express their sexuality.

As a middle-aged woman, thick around the middle, in my prime and not getting any younger or prettier, this is no time to reject the few opportunities that present themselves on a temporary basis. As my friend Kate would say, "I haven't had sex since the president was white!" (Trump is orange) Have they changed it?! (Asking for a friend) Still, I myself need more of an emotional bond before taking my clothes off. While friends have helped me to see it's not immoral to get your basic human needs met, I'm not so sure it's for me as I need to feel something. I (have and) can wait for someone who wants to put the effort into building something with me. I don't want to feel convenient for anyone. While I can't pretend to be pious, I do maintain a certain level of Catholic guilt despite my non-religious status. There are ways to protect yourself, however. While it's true no one can use you without your permission, there still should be some self-care rules so you don't wake up feeling like garbage the next morning.

First, this arrangement must be handled with respect. If a man were dating you, he'd likely bring you to a nice restaurant, mebbe some flowers (blech!), open doors for you, whatever. But this is not a date. He is under no obligation to woo you romantically. Wouldn't it be nice, though, if he were romantic nonetheless? Don't you deserve to be treated well, even if you're just bumping uglies temporarily? There is nothing wrong with having lunch first, or dinner afterward, hanging out to watch a movie, etc. If it's always "Wham bam, thank-you, Ma'am!" you just might feel like trash afterward. Choose a lover whom you have known for a long time — someone you truly consider a friend and trust whole-heartedly, not someone you recently met who is just looking for a convenient "friend" with benes. That man is likely never going to call you again after he gets what he came for.

This does not mean a married friend. Married people are off limits!! Just because you go in knowing he's not Mr. Right — he's Mr. (or Ms.) Right Now — doesn't mean you have any right to someone else's partner!! This is where you DO have to be ethical! Otherwise, you are only inviting pain and guilt into at least one other life, and very unnecessarily. A man claiming an 'open marriage' is still married — things can still get messy!! (But hey, if this is your thing, free feel!)

As I've said, if a guy friend tells you he can't sleep with you because he doesn't want to ruin the friendship, you can almost bet your next paycheck he is lying! If a guy is attracted to you, he will want to do you, come what may! Believe it! If, however, you approach him for a FWB agreement and he responds this way, respect that he isn't interested and just doesn't want to hurt your feelings. Hey, you've still got a friend <shrug>.

This is a verbal contract, not a one-night stand. Of course if a partner isn't happy with the results of the arrangement after the fact, you need to communicate that. Otherwise, you should assume this is an ongoing arrangement. Still, be prepared for the possibility that the friend who agreed to this arrangement just may bail on you soon afterward for whatever reason. That's the risk you take when there's no real commitment involved, and no true love holding you both there.

You should never speak of your other love interests! Just because this isn't love, that doesn't mean your verbally-contracted partner wants to hear about the feelings you may have for someone else, or about the other FWB partner(s) you're sharing yourself with. Unless you think hearing about the others would keep you (from falling in love) in check, let your FWB partner know it's not kewl to speak of any others until you develop that level of friendship and trust! It would be nice if you could dissolve the agreement being happy that your FWB partner found someone special to be in love with.

...Which brings me to safety measures, i.e. condoms. Protect yourself from disease! You don't know where that person has been, or where s/he's going, so give strong consideration to wearing a condom even if you're beyond the child-bearing years. Remember, you are essentially sleeping with everyone else that person has been with, and you have an obligation to protect your partner for the same reason(s).

As mentioned earlier, try to spend time outside of the bedroom now and then! Start with drinks, dinner, whatever! This will build a deeper intimacy with your FWB partner, and in this way it isn't just about the sex. Your relationship is a true friendship that's happily become more intimate. You are closer friends, not pieces of meat. The arrangement can get old fast if you start to feel convenient.

Deciding when you will get together should be a mutual thing, not just when the guy is available. If you are at his beck and call, he will likely lose respect and treat you like the back-burner fodder you allowed yourself to be. It's OK to say 'No, I'm not available tonight. How about tomorrow?' Women are more likely to clear their schedule to accommodate a man. You are not obligated to rearrange your life for anyone, especially not someone who isn't serious about you being in his life. Making yourself so available every time he wants you is a surefire way to feel like garbage about this arrangement. S/he likely isn't going anywhere if you say, "Sorry, not tonight."

If anything seems too personal, i.e. kissing, which might cause you to develop feelings of deeper love here, then don't do it! Getting emotionally involved can be a painful deal breaker! Otherwise, don't deny yourself that amazing passion. Kissing is where it all starts! YOU set the limits for your own comfort level.

It can be hard crossing the line of friendship initially. For your first time getting undressed, you may want to start with a "safe" position. For example, most old-fashioned women want to be made love to. Missionary might be a good position for such a woman to start with, moving on to more creative positions after that intimate trust is built (this is important!). If it's raging sex you both want, then hey, go for it! But if you're treading lightly, start slow with a safe but passionate position. Wine helps.

You should make it a point to talk the next day too — the day-after call. If this isn't available to you, at least talk about what happened immediately after the fact so you can be sure you're both still on the same page. If the sex was lousy for one of you, getting an honest answer might not be easy, but there's no better time to read body language than while yer still neked, eh?

Finally, be mentally prepared for a sudden dissolution of the contract. It's inevitable that one of you will eventually tire of the arrangement, or meet someone you are interested in for more than friendship. Good friends can endure this break-up, but others may find it awkward, at least initially. You must remind yourself it was just a matter of time, this wasn't love, and wish him/her well. You will likely not stay in touch immediately after that, only because the nature of the relationship has changed so drastically. As Dr. Seuss is credited with saying, "Don't cry because it's over; smile because it happened!" Or this one, for whom I don't know who to credit, "Sometimes good things fall apart so better things can fall together." If you are the one left alone, be confident it's just a matter of time before you're not alone again.

Being alone with your thoughts can be a very good, healthy thing! Allow yourself to be alone; sit with your feelings and explore them. What lessons did you learn? How was having this FWB arrangement a very positive experience? What would you do differently with someone else? Given the right circumstances, would you do this again?

All friendships can experience a drawback at any time. We get busy with our lives, moving on in various ways for a multitude of reasons. As my friend Todd says, "It's not that you're no longer friends, you just no longer have the same level of concern for each other." It's not personal, it's not right or wrong, it just is. If things peter out, so be it. It's sad, but life gets in the way and friendships change. As John Lennon sang, "Life is what happens while you're busy making other plans." Best to live in the present moment.

If you try an FWB arrangement and find it's not for you, no problem! Hey, you tried.

Expectations

I never believed I'd meet the man of my dreams sitting in a bar, and still don't. When women tell me they're divorcing their husband because he drinks and smokes, I remind them, "He was drinking and smoking in a bar when you met him. What did you expect?!" I also don't believe I'll meet the man of my dreams in a personal ad (unless of course Michael Sharp really does exist and is reading this. Call me!).

I'm still in contact with my twelfth-grade high school English teacher, Mrs. Siperstein. She is a wise woman who once told me, "There is no such thing as the perfect person because none of us is perfect! The trick to marrying the perfect person for you, then, is to find someone whose faults you can live with." Seems reasonable, right? Good, sound advice in this imperfect world! I'm not going to marry the first guy who doesn't piss me off, though. I'm not even sure I want to be married. I don't feel the need to own the piece of paper or the person, but I also don't like the idea of having a cynical mind, so I remain open to anything. I'd like to know it's an option though — to have someone love me enough to marry me if/when it matters. I like the idea of having my own space, and him having his — a retreat when we're just not in the mood to see each other. Lawd knows I'm not perfect, by any means. I just haven't found anyone whose faults I can live with. I'm not even sure what faults I am willing to live with, should I find someone I'm so compatible with. "They" say you'll know it when you find it, and I do believe that. We always tend to be better people when we meet 'The One', which is why the other person is often referred to as "my better half"!

Expectations. We get set in our ways as we get older, and that's pretty much where I'm at. I find the older I get, the more appealing it is to be alone. I don't really believe that's what I want, though. I prefer to think I'm going about my life doing what I love, patiently waiting for Mr. Right to come along. Serial dating is not very appealing to me at this point, and I'm not interested in Mr. Right Now. As alluded to previously, I would much rather drive to see Mr. Right than to have several Not-So-Rights close to home. At press time, I've still not found *him* near or far. The hope still exists, however, and who knows — mebbe he's reading this right now and will look me up! Stay tuned, I just might have to write the sequel to this book! Still, I go into these things with zero expectations as I find it generally leads to disappointment.

I've got lots of dating experience, even experience in marriage, but there isn't much you can do 'til the right one comes along. Be patient. Take up a new hobby, place yourself where like-minded people will be. They say "It's always when you're not looking!" I wasn't looking for 15 years while I raised my daughter alone, and now that I'm back out there, I find it's slim pickins.

Sometimes in online dating ads, the seekers will contact you from the other side of the country — even the other side of the world! I do know people who've taken the chance, met and eventually married that person in another state! Eventually, though, the long-distance thing is hard to do. Yes, it can be done, but you'd have to really be into the person for it to work. It does happen!

I'm older and know what I want. I'm constantly torn between "Don't settle!" and "You ain't gettin' any younger! Give the fat little bald guy a chance!" Of course this is the advice I get from friends who didn't settle, and found themselves a heartthrob — the love of their life! Yes, give folks a chance, but don't settle! You deserve true happiness! When it's right, you know it! I've not given up on the dream. I'm next!! ☺

Utilize the power of intention. You know what you want, so put it out there! The Universe is listening. Pray, meditate, journal — whatever it is you need to do to put it out there — and without expectations! Be aware of the energy you emit; you may think you're ready for a LTR, but if there's a blockage (conscious or not), people will sense it and you don't have a prayer. If you are truly clear for a new relationship, truly want this right now, your energy will tell the world as much! And then don't just sit around waiting for it to fall into your lap — go get it! If you're sitting at a park bench and Mr./Ms. Right comes and sits next to you, you are presented with a choice. Will you strike up a conversation, or be two ships passing in the night? The Universe can only do so much; the rest is up to you.

Hope springs eternal in the human breast...
~Alexander Pope

Unless this book is a flaming success and I need more material, I'm done with online dating. Kudos to all my friends who've met and married the partner of their dreams — it does happen! However, I'm convinced I'll meet someone the old-fashioned way — going about my business, doing what I enjoy, and then *POOF!*, he'll *appear* when I'm not looking.

I'm still holding out hope anyway. Every day above ground is a second chance! While I remain whole-heartedly *not* in love, I am still vehemently hopeful.

This is my life...
My story... my book.
I will no longer let
Anyone else write it;
Nor will I apologize for the edits I make
~Steve Maraboli

275

Booty Calls

In this day and age of folks not wanting to marry or commit fully, entering into a Friends With Benefits agreement seems the best way to remain single and free while getting your carnal needs met. But if you're looking for something more short-lived, it's just a booty call you want. Online dating sites seem to be the perfect place to find your next booty call, be it one night or more. To avoid the booty callers, some people (male and female) will put in their profile the disclaimer that "I'm not looking for a one-night stand; I'm looking for something real." This seems to be an all-call for booty callers to accept the challenge of calling them out if they're covering, or converting them if they're legit in their desire to find a long-term relationship.

Barring all those who truly are highly principled and are perfectly willing to wait for someone special, some egotistical beings tend to think they'll be the one to lure out this commitment-minded person for a night. If it progresses beyond that, great. Just don't be so quick to settle, or to sell yourself. You're an adult, but be smart about it. Eyes wide open!

Again — be forewarned. Not everyone who says s/he's looking for a LTR is sincere. Women want to know a guy is looking for a LTR, so men say it. Many of these meetings start with the desire for a booty call, nothing more. If something more should come of it <ahem>, great — but take your time if it's a LTR you're looking for! Remember, while it seems most everyone expects to be in bed by the second or third date these days, it's still a rule never never on the first date, lest they think you're too easy!

One more thought on this. While a man will eagerly bed you, that doesn't mean he wants to keep you. If you make the choice to bed a man on the first date because you believe things are going so well, don't expect a call the next day — an age-old expectation, not a new rule! If you go in on the first date knowing the deal, you are either in need of the attention, or in sabotage mode. You know he's not right for you, so you hope he doesn't call again. Still, emotionless ex can be very difficult for some women.

When you do hope he'll call, but he doesn't, it can be maddening for sure. You sit there thinking, We had a great time, why doesn't he want me? I'm attractive enough, I'm smart enough, successful enough, fun enough, and we have this great chemistry! Why am I not enough?! You *are* enough, you just aren't what he wants. You will be enough for the right person — someone who appreciates you!!

Thoughts on Marriage

Men know! I've heard several stories of men seeing their woman for the first time and saying, "Oh my god, I'm gonna marry that woman!" I don't often hear women saying the same thing, in fact quite the opposite — didn't want to give him the time of day at first, but glad they did! I don't know what it is, perhaps just the visual excitement of seeing a woman they find to be exactly what they want physically, as they haven't even talked to her yet. But it's a thing!

My ex-husband Ernie said this happened for him. At the time, I was dating his friend Paul and wouldn't have given him a second look otherwise. One day, Paul said to me, "Ernie wants to know if you'll go out with him." Huh? I just looked at him with that deer in the headlights show of non-comprehension for a few silent moments. "Um, but I'm with you!" I uttered. "I know," said Paul, "but he told me to ask you, so I'm asking." I thought that was the end of it, but like a fox waiting for sick chickens, checking in occasionally for the right time to pounce, Ernie caught me a couple of years later at a vulnerable time. This was well after Paul and I had broken things off, and I gave him a chance. He was much more attractive at that point, having gained weight after returning from active military duty. He was a very good-looking guy. Strange, he reminded me of Jeffrey Dahmer, only he wouldn't eat me. But I digress. At the time, you could not have convinced me I would ever marry him. In fact, I am still in disbelief.

After a year of living together, I think he knew I had one foot out the door and made a desperate plea for my hand. When he gave his heartfelt proposal, I thought, Wow! No one would ever love me as much as he does (I later learned he was co-dependent. Clinginess should've been a sign, but I was oh so young), so I said Yes. The first year was great, kids playing house! But when I decided I wanted a place to call our own, and a real bed instead of an old mattress on the floor, S#!t got real. He couldn't handle it, and I could see it as clearly as body parts through plastic wrap at a Mazola party. (The marriage is now just a blur though.)

I ended things in our second year of marriage. His ability to initially say, "That's Wifey right there!" didn't equate to *keeping* me his wife. Knowing I was ready to leave, he begged me for a baby. I reminded him, "You need two things to have a baby: a job, and sex. And you have neither, so…"

You need at least a year to see a person through all his/her seasons, even better if it's two years, as it's easy to play the game for just a year, hiding true colors. Although I'd known my husband before marrying him, even lived with him for a year, I didn't see his true colors until the fourth year. Like Maria sings in The Sound of Music — Wait a year or two! If you must be engaged after the first year — the point at which some women start demanding a major commitment — take a year to plan the wedding!

Lots of couples are content without the piece of paper. Is it that important to you? If so, and you knew each other previously — there are no secrets — then hey, go for it! While marriage isn't for everyone, some folks really want to be married! The young have lots of time and can afford to wait. When you truly know what you want, it makes it so much easier to say no to what you don't want. So when you find what you want, why not tie the knot? <Shrug> I'm just a firm believer in giving it time to be sure it's right. The pain of divorce isn't pretty.

I cringe when I hear people announce an engagement with someone they've known for just a few months. Some people really do know it in their hearts that they've found the right one and want to rush to the altar. Fine; put a ring on it. Generally speaking though, even if you're going in with eyes wide open, you need at least a year to see someone through all his/her seasons. You, too, can be fooled past the one-year mark — as I was. Some people are very talented at hiding their true colors.

What's the big rush? We may not be getting any younger or prettier, but you've still got the rest of your life to be (hopefully) happily married. Allow yourself this time to really be sure.

There's an expression, *Women marry men hoping they'll change; men marry women hoping they won't.* This expression holds true. I'm not the same person I was at 18, or when I was 25, or when I was 34... I've been a work in progress and salute my many changes. While I hope to continue to grow in many ways, I can't imagine I will change at the very core. It took me all these years to figure out who I am and what I want — but now I know! If only I could have all this knowledge in my 18-year-old body.

They say couples sorta start to look alike after living together awhile. My theory is that they always looked alike, which is why they were attracted to each other in the first place! An unconscious narcissism thing. They recognized something familiar in the other person— like seeing yourself in a mirror — and were instantly attracted. No wonder they look so cute together!

I never understood getting married a virgin. I understand the religious aspect. It's insurance you won't compare your man to another. Think about it — in biblical times, it was very much a man's world and they made the rules (think cavemen, dragging you by the hair — "You! You are my wombman!"). It stands to reason they would want a woman to only have one lover so she'd have no one to compare him to. She might've spent her entire life thinking 'that's it', good or bad. But now we women have options without the judgment. Try a sample before committing! I personally think people should have leases instead of marriages, like when you go car shopping. I want to kick the tires first. Sign a two-year contract, ride it for a while. At the designated time, if you don't feel like riding it anymore, cut it loose (you may have to pay a bit if it's all dinged and scratched up). Otherwise, you get to ride it some more. You may decide it's not working out for ya, or you just might choose to keep it for the long haul, drive it into the ground. My friends tell me I'll buy when I find the right one.

free Advice & final Thoughts

It seems like the same people stay on the same sites for a very long time — years even! Yet still they are holding out for perfection (or using the sites as a pool for fresh meat). Good for these men (I can't speak for the women since I don't check out their ads) as they are not settling, I guess, but it got me thinking.

When your ad first goes live, you get inundated with responses of all kinds (FRESH MEAT!). Eventually, that comes to an end, and you don't get any responses. You can try changing your primary photo as most people just look at that and make a snap decision whether or not to look at your ad further.

At one point in my journey, I wondered what would happen if I changed my Body Type answer in my ad profile. Surely all those hot guys who weren't contacting me were looking for the svelte women. I clicked off of 'A Few Extra Pounds' and moved it to 'Average'. That same day I got several people wanting to meet me, some adding me to their Favorites list, but only just a few actual messages (most of which were from guys who live in mommy's basement).

Then I changed my body type to 'Athletic', and guess what? Message explosion! What's ironic about this, though, most of the people who messaged me were older and overweight! These men had not contacted me before, only when they thought I had a great body. What gives? Do they really think that if I'm all that, they could have me? Ah yes, the high school football hero in their mind does! I think it's important to keep your expectations real.

And where are all the 'Athletic' men looking for someone my age? Checking out the younger women! Younger, shorter, prettier, more money? Seems like the more perfect the man, the more infallible the Barbie must be. Stands to reason, though. If a man is fit at an older age, he wants a younger woman, whether looking to father children or not. It's in his wiring — a Darwinian thing. You can write to him and hope for the best, but don't hold your breath. He prolly ain't writin' back.

Sigmund Freud believed women have penis envy. I think he may've been onto something there, but not for the more obvious reason. Women don't wish we carried junk between our legs instead of on our chests; we wish we could be more like the guys since they seem to have the upper hand in matters of the heart! What if women changed the game? What if we used the same lines on men that they use on us? "You don't have to do anything you don't want to… I have to be up early in the morning… I'll call you…"

Roles are changing! Men don't know what their role is any longer. What is it? A free-for-all, anything goes?? Gone are the days when it's solely the woman's job to cook, clean and take care of the kids. It's rare, I think, to find a man who brings flowers on the first date, pulls out a chair for the lady, pays the tab most of the time, does all the calling. When I was a kid, a lady would never dream of calling the man, planning the date, etc. Now I think men expect, or at least hope, the woman will text him if she is interested so he doesn't have to guess or do all the work. None of this old-fashioned gentleman stuff! I've given many examples of men who not only didn't drop a dime on coffee but left me with the tab!

And with online dating making people so accessible, booty calls are on the rise while relationships and marriages are on the decline. Only when a true fire ignites do we get past the first date into something meaningful these days. Relationships take work, whereas being single is easy. None of the burdens of having to put forth effort when you can just take a booty call to tide you over till the next trieste.

Some people honestly do not know how to be a good partner. Some of us are so used to dysfunctional relationships, we wouldn't know healthy if it bit us in the arse. You may tell yourself you're a good person — and you are! But having once held an official marriage certificate — being experienced in marriage — doesn't mean you were successful at it. Let's face it, divorce wouldn't be an epidemic if we were so good at being partners! It's not anyone else's job to make me happy. That comes from within, and putting effort into a relationship comes from without. It's not 50/50, effort is 100/100! Communication is the key. If you don't know what your partner needs or wants, ASK! If you aren't getting what you need or want, ASK!! And if you do something wrong, apologize! I have no problem admitting when I'm wrong. Like that time I got married just for shits & giggles.

Social media is one of the worst things we could've done to our society. OK, aside from Global Warming. Lonely people go on Facebook looking to be entertained, to take a little boredom out of their day, but what they sometimes find just makes matters worse. We see other people venting, airing their dirty laundry, raising our shackles if we take certain things personally. It can be very time-consuming, like having a part-time job! This is so counterproductive to our overall healthy moods, when we could've been out kayaking, or basking in the sun with a good book. This is why people occasionally choose to take a break from social media sites, often dismantling their accounts because they take things to heart and know they can't handle the strain. I've done it myself. There are certain things I just don't need to see when I'm feeling a bit 'off'. Nor do I want anything killing my mood when I'm feelin' fine!

Our kids don't know how to function without their electronics. While holding a phone in their hands, they prefer to text their friends rather than hear a live voice! Why not just type a half sentence of symbols? It's so much faster! (UGH!) As a result, not only are they losing ground in school, they don't learn how to effectively communicate with other humans. What will dating be like for them? What will our society be like if we forget basic human communication?! Actually, some 'onliners' just want to text all the time, in which case this could work out for them. However, this could result in a serious decline in the population.

While it's easy to fall in love, a great love is hard to find. I firmly believe men only love that way once! Just like Smokey Robinson sang:

> *Although she might be cute,*
> *she's just a substitute*
> *because you're the permanent one.*

I also like this — How Much I Feel by Ambrosia:

I've got a wife now, years we've been goin' strong.
There's just something that I've got to say.
Sometimes when we make love, I still see your face.

Addiction to the attraction phase prevents people from having a healthy relationship with a partner who is probably a really great catch. After the breakup, you feel like it was a great ride — nice while it lasted but it's over now (usually around the 3-month mark), time to get off. Things can crash and burn, making it feel like it wasn't so special after all. If we hadn't been looking for this instant love, we wouldn't have been so vulnerable and blind. We are, in essence, guilty for wanting and taking the drug. Coming down from the high is no fun. There's something to be said for going slowly, building a solid base of friendship and knowing what you're getting upfront.

A friend once told me every guy secretly wishes his woman would call him daddy, "and don't let them tell you otherwise!" I gave it some thought and I guess it makes sense. Considering the Oedipus complex, Freud's theory that boys desire to (but ought not to) sleep with their mother, this is the flip side. It's unthinkable for a man to lay with his daughter (in 47 states anyway), so we're just talking male fantasy here. I later remembered I once had an old boyfriend ask me to call him daddy during a lovemaking session and so I did it for the moment. I made sure to ask him about it later, but he immediately shut the conversation down and it never came up again. Most humans aren't comfortable speaking about quirks in their sexual desires.

When it comes to sex, I'm pretty straight-laced. I never felt the need to throw in some extra people or crazy toys, and pain is definitely off limits. But I understand the clinical reasons why some people do like pain. It comes from the same center of your brain where pleasure comes from. I just never derived pleasure from pain myself. (inflicting it might be a different matter, haha!) If that's your thing, you can find a discreet way to put that into your ad to attract a particular kind of lover. There's also probably a website just for you.

If you're going to tell a woman about your porn collection, or your penchant for online pornography (or she finds out accidentally), you need to open that conversation. Let her know that you would gladly include her in this if she is open to it, but assure her it doesn't mean you've lost interest in her! Women like to feel like they are enough for you. It's hard to comprehend why you need to look at other women when you say you are attracted to her. Catching you sneaking porn at 3:00 in the morning not only makes it look like you are sneaking an emotional affair, it's a major ego crusher for her. Mebbe a sweet, old-fashioned guy doesn't have the least bit interest in porn whether his partner is satisfying him or not, but he's likely not as creative in bed either (You can use this in yer argument!). If you are going to open up to your partner about your penchant for porn, you had better be ready to defend yourself in a way she can accept.

Men are not monogamous by nature; women usually are. Plus, we figure you agreed to a commitment, so there are to be no other women—emotional or otherwise! A clued-in woman understands, and may accept his roving eye to some degree, but she still expects him to keep his pants on (without argument!). Overall, if you are sexually active you had better make her feel like she is it.

Variety is the spice of life, and a man's gotta eat! (Peruse the buffet, but eat at home!) Things can get a bit stale when you've been together awhile. I believe we have a duty to keep things alive in the bedroom (so take it outside the bedroom now and then!). It's easy to let that intimacy, which is oh-so important, fall to the wayside — especially if we are busy with work, kids, and just daily life in general. Date night is a great place to start! Spice the romance up a bit to keep your partner interested! Otherwise, s/he may go sniffing elsewhere once the ark docks.

I've said cheating, in my humble opinion, is a character flaw. Women, especially, don't usually burn their bridges until they're on the other side. If she's faithful to her affair, she's got an agenda. When she leaves her husband, it's because she was ready to do so and there will be no looking back. This doesn't mean she isn't looking forward to her next affair though. That character flaw — in a man or a woman — hasn't gone away, it's just hiding, waiting to resurface once the excitement wears off (or the money runs out!).

Feeling wronged by someone? What goes around comes around. Like my grandmother used to say, "All you have to do is sit back and *wait*." I wish no ill will on anyone, I just think you get what you put out there. The Universe has a system of checks and balances. Put out loving, positive vibes, people!

Rebounders abound! Your ex may not necessarily want you back, but s/he doesn't want you being happy in love with someone else, either. This is what being "on the rebound" is usually about. You start seeing someone new and they get wind of it, they either harass the hell out of you or make a play to get you back. Of course once they do get you back, you have the same old problems, and they can't kick you to the curb fast enough. See it for what it is and *just say no!*

Just because he brought you home to meet the parents/family doesn't mean you're "in". That's more likely to be true if a woman brings you home to meet the family. How a man reacts to this invitation may also be very telling of how serious he is about you (not to be confused with nerves as this can be a harrowing experience for anyone!). I find it's best to save that noise till you get past the dreaded three-month mark. My dad used to say, "Don't bring him home unless it's very serious!" My thoughts exacalackily!

In a perfect world, men would just be upfront about their need for sex. "Look, you're a great gal, I'm just not into you for keeps. If you wanna bump uglies, I'm here for you tonight. Mebbe tomorrow night too, if my guys aren't around." But no, they've gotta play the game. Don't hate the player, hate the game? He can't make you a pawn without your permission. Choose not to play the game! Call him (or her!) out on that noise!

Men lie. Women lie too. I can't stress this enough — If a person wants to be with you, there will be no excuses! Nothing will keep him/her from being with you!! Take the hint and move on. Whether or not you want to jump into bed with someone who isn't interested in anything more — and spells that out for you right upfront — is your decision, but go in with eyes wide open. There are none so blind as those who don't want to see! I now look for men who are brutally honest. I'd much rather tolerate some haughtiness than lies.

Some guys are tired of failure and will do anything to make a relationship last, even though the divisiveness is on the wall. Is suffering through a bad relationship really the answer? You're not going to change anything that way. Yes, you will be alone, but! You won't be in a miserable relationship. You'll be making room for a healthy one! You can't write the next chapter of your life if you keep re-reading the last one.

I'm always amazed when perfect strangers write for the sole purpose of calling you out on something stoopid! A young man once contacted me to trash me for still running my ad after only five months (This isn't even a long time considering other ads I've seen running for years!). Poor boy, he had no idea with whom he was dealing. I responded thusly. "Thank you for bring-ing this to my attention. I actually started seeing someone special last month and completely forgot to take down my ad, having not been on the site all this time. I see that your ad is still running though. Perhaps if you didn't have such a negative attitude, you'd find someone special too. Good luck with that." He did not reply.

Another man said I look far younger than my stated age, so I must be using old photos! I assured him they were current, but he couldn't let it go! I could tell from his tone that he wasn't interested in dating me, so clearly he was just looking to call me out on his suspicion that I was lying about my photos. Do people lay awake at night worrying about this stuff?! If you don't want to date me, DON'T! It's that simple. You don't know me, Pal! Mebbe if you weren't (a total tool) so bitter and argumentative (manopause?) you'd have a woman! NEXT!

Most of us wait for things to happen. But when we do this, almost always something bad happens! Why not make GOOD things happen?! Don't wait for a special occasion to break out the good China — TODAY is special! Enjoy your NOW since you're not promised beyond. In the immortal words of Van Halen, Do it right here and Now. Right now!

> *Right now, hey, it's your tomorrow.*
> *Right now, c'mon, it's everything!*
> *Right now, catch a magic moment—*
> *Do it right here and now.*
> *It means everything!*
> *Miss the beat, you lose the rhythm*
> *And nothing falls into place*

My friend Kevin, who is now the proprietor of an English language learners school in Asia, didn't wait for life to happen. Things changed drastically for him when he started conversing with a woman in Thailand several years ago.

"After three days of talking about 20 hours a day, I said, 'I'm coming to see you.' Of course she said I'm crazy and didn't believe me but I bought a ticket and flew to Asia. All my brothers thought I would have my kidney stolen. I showed up in time for Valentine's Day, which is also her birthday. So romantic, I want to puke when I think about it now. But we have created an empire so I guess we did something right."

We could get hit by a bus tomorrow; disease isn't selective... Do whatever it is that makes you happy!

People are always amazed when they discover I'm a comedian. "You?! But you're so serious!" BAHAHAHAHA. Truth be told, I'm a very private person and don't feel the need to divulge too much to strangers, or even coworkers unless they express an interest in my personal life. Invariably, the next comment is, "Tell me a joke!" To this I say, "Pay me!" I'm a professional; that $h!t ain't free! Why do people assume it's my job to make them laugh simply because I can?! Hell, I'm not always 'on'. Sometimes I *am* rather serious! I would never dream of asking someone to perform his job for me! Oh, so sorry, I'm off the clock right now!!

Remember the band Procol Harum? The term is adapted from the Latin *beyond these things*. There was much controversy over the song Whiter Shade of Pale, but they didn't feel the need to explain.

One of my biggest pet peeves is how everyone automatically misspells Alison. No matter how many times I start off by saying, "It's Alison with one 'L'. A-L-I-S..., they STILL spell it with two L's! Welcome to my Theatre of Pay Attention!! It's been Alison for 500 years. Suddenly, everyone has to be creative, and now I can't get a toothbrush with my name on it! The name is not pronounced ALL-ison, it's AL! I once got a credit card with my name erroneously spelled with two L's and complained. The agent sucked her teeth at me and said, "Close enough!" (face palm) Ah, no, I don't think so!! This is legal paperwork I'll be signing

292

each time you want my money. You want to do business with me? Spell my name correctly!!

You want to score points within your relationships? Listen to what the other person is saying — really LISTEN! And look beyond these things — the little things.

Often when we start a new relationship, we sometimes see only the good qualities. The person just doesn't seem to have any bad ones. This temporary state of perfection is you putting that person on a pedestal. As long as we remember *nobody's perfect*, the pedestal phase can be enjoyed for what it is — a phase. A grace period. It's when we actually believe our own projection that madness ensues. When you put someone on a pedestal, you are giving away your power and saying you're not good enough. These people are not gods. You, however, are a goddess! Never, ever, lower yourself for anyone!

Dad's Definition of Love

From the time I was a little girl of about ten, my dad started telling me what he thought love is. Over the years, he added on to his definition, so that by the time I was a Communications/Journalist/English major in college, he felt he could write a book on the subject, and made me promise to help him write it before he died (not that he was dying any time soon). I said I would, but it was really just a long list of nouns, adjectives and verbs which he never got around to writing down for me. I'm going by memory, so it's not going to be nearly half as long as Dad's list was. It's mostly common sense anyway, but, a promise is a promise! So here it is, Daddy. I've kept all my promises to you now! Semper Fi! ♥

Love is: giving, receiving, caring, compassion, sharing, communication, acceptance, sacrifice, understanding, feeling, tender, unconditional, hopeful, protective, dependable, making concessions, listening, affection, pleasure, attraction, persevering, not proud, kind, supportive, patient, positive, unselfish, trusting, wanting, being present

About the Author

A lison O'Donnell was accidentally born in Connecticut, but is a life-long native Rhode Islander. A self-proclaimed adrenaline junkie, Alison has been skydiving, bungee jumping, hot air ballooning, scuba diving with sharks, zip lining, exceeding the speed limit halfway around the world, and is the mother of one teenage daughter. She received a Bachelor of Arts in Mass Communications from Rhode Island College, a Secondary English teacher certification from Providence College, and a Master's from the school of hard knocks. A creature of the stage, she has performed comedy in the Southern New England area for more than half her life, and played with various local bands as a singer/musician. In her spare time, Alison enjoys hiking with her two bichons, Rhett and Scarlett. She has taught high school English for the past 17 years, and doesn't really know what she wants to be when she grows up.

84068249R00173

Made in the USA
San Bernardino, CA
03 August 2018